THE COLORADO PLATEAU

THE LAND

and

THE INDIANS

NATIONAL PARKS AND MONUMENTS

ARCHES NATIONAL PARK, UTAH
AZTEC RUINS NATIONAL MONUMENT, NEW MEXICO
BANDELIER NATIONAL MONUMENT, NEW MEXICO
BLACK CANYON OF THE GUNNISON NATIONAL MONUMENT,
COLORADO
BRYCE CANYON NATIONAL PARK, UTAH
CANYON DE CHELLY NATIONAL MONUMENT, ARIZONA
CANYONLANDS NATIONAL PARK, UTAH
CAPITOL REEF NATIONAL PARK, UTAH
CEDAR BREAKS NATIONAL MONUMENT, UTAH
CHACO CULTURE NATIONAL HISTORICAL PARK, NEW MEXICO
COLORADO NATIONAL MONUMENT, COLORADO
CURECANTI NATIONAL RECREATIONAL AREA, COLORADO
DINOSAUR NATIONAL MONUMENT, COLORADO-UTAH
EL MORRO NATIONAL MONUMENT, NEW MEXICO
EL MALPAIS NATIONAL MONUMENT, NEW MEXICO
FORT UNION NATIONAL MONUMENT, NEW MEXICO
GLEN CANYON NATIONAL RECREATION AREA, UTAH
GRAND CANYON NATIONAL PARK, ARIZONA,
GREAT SAND DUNES NATIONAL MONUMENT, COLORADO
HOVENWEEP NATIONAL MONUMENT, COLORADO-UTAH
HUBBEL TRADING POST NATIONAL HISTORICAL SITE, ARIZONA
LAKE MEAD NATIONAL RECREATION AREA, ARIZONA-NEVADA
MESA VERDE NATIONAL PARK, COLORADO
MONTEZUMA CASTLE NATIONAL MONUMENT, ARIZONA
NAVAJO NATIONAL MONUMENT, ARIZONA
NATURAL BRIDGES NATIONAL MONUMENT, UTAH
PECOS NATIONAL HISTORICAL PARK, NEW MEXICO
PETRIFIED FOREST NATIONAL PARK (INCLUDES PAINTED DESERT
OVERLOOK), ARIZONA
PETROGLYPH NATIONAL MONUMENT, NEW MEXICO
PIPE SPRINGS NATIONAL MONUMENT, ARIZONA
RAINBOW BRIDGE NATIONAL MONUMENT, UTAH
SALINAS PUEBLO MISSIONS NATIONAL MONUMENT, NEW MEXICO
SUNSET CRATER NATIONAL MONUMENT, ARIZONA
TUZIGOOT NATIONAL MONUMENT, ARIZONA
WALNUT CANYON NATIONAL MONUMENT, ARIZONA
WUPATKI NATIONAL MONUMENT, ARIZONA
YUCCA HOUSE NATIONAL MONUMENT, COLORADO
ZION NATIONAL PARK, UTAH
ZUNI-CÍBOLA NATIONAL HISTORICAL PARK, NEW MEXICO

*FRONT COVER: LIGHTNING, MONUMENT VALLEY NAVAJO
TRIBAL PARK, ARIZONA-UTAH*

OPPOSITE PAGE: BALANCED ROCK, ARCHES NATIONAL PARK, UTAH

THIS PAGE: BRYCE CANYON NATIONAL PARK, UTAH

*INSIDE BACK COVER: COLORADO RIVER,
CANYONLANDS NATIONAL PARK, UTAH*

*BACK COVER: TURRET ARCH WITH HALE-BOPP COMET, ARCHES NATIONAL
PARK, UTAH*

THE COLORADO

THE LAND

ARCHES NATIONAL PARK, UTAH

TOP: RAINBOW BRIDGE NATIONAL MONUMENT, UTAH

MIDDLE: PETRIFIED LOG, PETRIFIED FOREST NATIONAL PARK, ARIZONA

BOTTOM: DINOSAUR TRACKS, MOENAVE FORMATION, HURRICANE CLIFTS, UTAH

Copyright 1999
**Thunder Mesa
Publishing, Inc.**
208 Sherwood Boulevard
Los Alamos, New Mexico 87544
505-672-3108 • FAX 505-672-0231
ALL RIGHTS RESERVED

PLATEAU

THE INDIANS

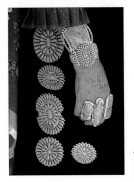

ZUNI DANCER, GALLUP INTERTRIBAL INDIAN CEREMONIAL, GALLUP, NEW MEXICO

TOP: WUPATKI RUIN, WAPATKI NATIONAL MONUMENT, ARIZONA

MIDDLE: TUZIGOOT NATIONAL MONUMENT, ARIZONA

BOTTOM: SALINAS PUEBLO MISSIONS NATIONAL MONUMENT, NEW MEXICO

Text By: Kathleene Parker, Thunder Mesa Publishing, Inc.

Photographs By: Tom Till, Moab, Utah

Additional Photographs By: Stephen Trimble, Salt Lake City, Utah

Edited By: K. C. Compton, Casper, Wyoming

Design By: Candus O. Clark and Kathleene Parker
Graphics By: Candus O. Clark, Sunburst Graphics & Printing, Inc.

Comptroller: Mel Burnett

Printing By: Kings Time Printing Press Ltd., Hong Kong

Introduction

This is Indian country, here in the depths of the desert and mountains of Colorado, Utah, Arizona, and New Mexico—the Four Corners states, a land of sculptured rock and distant lavender mesas, of windswept arroyos, cactuses, of silence, and the unhurried flow of time.

This is the heartland of the American West, certainly of the American Southwest—a land that melds legends of cowboys and Indians, missionaries and outlaws, a land of relentless sun and seemingly endless miles between remote desert towns.

Gallup, Holbrook, Cortez, Green River, Winslow—towns with names that slip off the tongue like the whispered loneliness of a distant train whistle at midnight.

Legends were born here amid the towering bluffs and buttes of Monument Valley and the twisted rocks of Canyonlands, in the depths of the Grand Canyon, and along the now mostly silent miles of Route 66,

WIGWAM MOTEL, OLD ROUTE 66, HOLBROOK, ARIZONA

not that long ago a well-traveled highway bordered by Burma Shave signs and billboards promising a Las Vegas casino to be ten miles closer than the last sun-blistered sign ten miles back.

This is Indian country of legend—and of myth, a land made larger than life by Western writers Zane Grey and Louise Lamour and the silver screen of Hollywood. But it is a land that in reality dwarfs even Hollywood's Technicolor® depiction of it.

Indian country, in large measure the expanses of the magnificent Colorado Plateau, is a land molded by nearly endless ages and the unparalleled forces of nature into one of the most remarkable landscapes on the planet.

The Colorado Plateau—actually a vast geologic province encompassing much of the Southwest—is a place where time and space interlock, with reminders of ten centuries past, a hundred centuries past, and ten thousand centuries past floating into today and just as ceaselessly into a million and ten million tomorrows.

To those accustomed to the greenness of gentler places, the Colorado Plateau may seem desolate and unwelcoming. But this is a land that should be cherished and revered on its own merits—not judged by the standards of other lands. Its beauty can seem ominous and sinister, but it is also a beauty of unreserved elegance, dominated by nature and the sweeping currents of time, not by humankind—perhaps the reason some feel so threatened and alone here.

But in the soft coolness after great, rumbling summer storms, ephemeral rainbows span mighty canyons, tiny hummingbirds sip nectar from flowers growing near desert seeps, and tablelands shimmer lavender in the heat-distorted distance. It is then the air carries a fragrance like none on Earth, a soft intermingling of piñon, sage, and just-fallen rain.

"And the air," late nineteenth century American author Wella Cather wrote in *The Professors House*, "My God, what air!—Soft, tingling, gold, hot with an edge of chill on it, full of the smell of piñons—it was like breathing the sun, breathing the colour of the sky."

And upon this extraordinary land live American Indians—sometimes called Native Americans—the indigenous people of the Colorado Plateau. Their cultures evolved here over thousands of years, cultures that stand out as brightly against the stark bluffs and buttes as bolts of lightning in a dark summer storm.

They are the Ute, Paiute, Navajo, Jicarilla Apache, Pai, and Pueblo peoples, distinct tribal groups with widely disparate histories, languages, religions, and customs.

They are people whose story is more mesmerizing and beautiful than fiction could ever be, people still individualistic, whose lives echo cultures reaching back centuries, even millennia, in this place. They are people molded by the domineering strength of a beautiful but unforgiving land, by an adversity that has made their cultures colorful and resilient and, perhaps inevitably, as intriguing as the land upon which they live.

THE LAND

NAVAJO, MONUMENT VALLEY NAVAJO TRIBAL PARK, ARIZONA-UTAH

The Colorado Plateau

On the border between Utah and Arizona, at the northern edge of the Navajo Nation and almost in the center of the Colorado Plateau, the towering bluffs and pinnacles of Monument Valley jut from a bright red land canopied by a turquoise sky.

In the Monument Valley Navajo Tribal Park, the buttes known as Left Mitten, Right Mitten, and Merrick Butte, or a little to the south, the towering pinnacles known as the Totem Pole and Yei-Bi-Chei—often seen with Navajos herding sheep nearby—are recognized symbols of the American West.

These and many other geologic features of Indian Country are a product of erosional forces of catastrophic proportions and of the influence of the primordial past.

The term Colorado Plateau refers not to a plateau in the conventional sense of the word, but to an enormous 150,000 square mile, roughly

PREVIOUS PAGE: CASTLE ROCK, NEAR MOAB, UTAH.

7

round geologic province, stretching from central Arizona's Mogollon Rim on the south, to northern Utah on the north, almost to the Nevada border on the west, and through southwest Colorado and northwest New Mexico to the Rio Grande on the east.

The Colorado Plateau is one of the most scenic and colorful regions in the world. Over thirty United States national parks and monuments—the Golden Circle of National Parks—rest upon its expanses. Many people have argued that, because of its spectacular beauty and geologic grandeur, the entire region should be protected as the Colorado Plateau National Park.

Four of the Colorado Plateau's parks, Mesa Verde and Grand Canyon national parks, Chaco Culture National Historical Park and Aztec Ruins National Monument number among a relative few places in the United State recognized by the United Nations Educational, Scientific, and Cultural Organization as World Heritage Sites, in consideration of natural and cultural features of global preeminence.

Taos Pueblo, just slightly beyond the eastern edge of the Colorado Plateau on a sagebrush-carpeted mesa at the base of the Sangre de Cristo Mountains, is also a World Heritage Site and the largest continually occupied multi-storied Indian pueblo in the United States.

Geologically, the Colorado Plateau is an anomaly, a surviving portion of the nuclear center—the craton—of a continent dating from a time long before there was a North America, to a time of the first flickering of life on the planet. The plateau is a huge segment of continental crust that has somehow survived relatively intact for over two billion years, a sanctuary from most geologic turmoil despite the chaos of folding, faulting, and mountain building that sometimes surrounded it.

In fact, the Colorado Plateau may have been spared the tumult due in part to the great thickness of rock amassed upon it during those unfathomably long ages, layer deposited upon layer as literally thousands of millions of years slipped by, until rock layers more than two miles thick had accumulated.

And because this land has survived relatively intact for so many ages, it represents a fascinating window into the Earth's geologic past. It is as if the plateau was chosen to be Nature's attic, a repository for the collective clutter of epochs reaching back to ages long before dinosaurs left their footprints along the edges of primeval bogs.

During the craton's long journey through time, it also traveled across much of the face of the Earth.

About 245 million years ago, the Earth's land masses—including the Colorado Plateau—were fused together into the sprawling supercontinent, Pangea.

But about 200 million years ago, Pangea began fragmenting under the forces of plate tectonics—the ploddingly slow but persistent movement of the continental plates over the Earth's mantle—into the land masses that eventually became the continents of today.

During and after the fragmentation of Pangea, ancestral North America—and with it the craton that is now the Colorado Plateau—moved from slightly south of the equator, where it had rested in a stable position for nearly 300 million years, and traveled slowly northward across roughly two thousand miles of the planet's surface.

Those long ages and long miles of travel through various latitudes and longitudes caused the craton to experience varying climates and

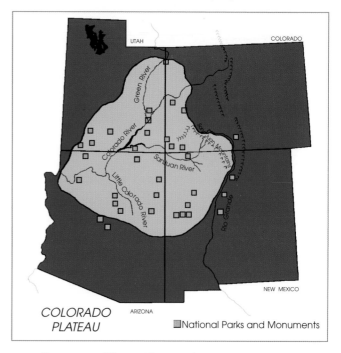

COLORADO PLATEAU

■ National Parks and Monuments

weather conditions. The region was alternatively inundated by seas, experienced the tropical dampness of the equatorial zones, the heat and drought of a Sahara-like desert, and then a more temperate climate as the craton moved across the Tropic of Cancer, northward to where it now rests roughly halfway between the equator and the North Pole.

But another spectacular accident of geology helped to shape the destiny of the Colorado Plateau.

Remnants of the distant past exist elsewhere on the planet, although often deeply hidden within the Earth, out of view of humankind. The Colorado Plateau realized its spectacular geologic destiny because, after hundreds of millions of years of resting relatively flat and undisturbed, the plateau, between five and ten million years ago—recently, in geologic time—began uplifting.

Like an enormous boil, the Colorado Plateau—for reasons geologists do not yet understand—

buckled slowly, inexorably upward, until it was thousands of feet higher than surrounding lands.

Even most of the plateau's lower regions now rest at over five thousand feet above sea level, and the peaks of its desert mountains reach ten thousand and twelve thousand feet.

Meanwhile, southwest Colorado's towering San Juan Mountains—by some definitions part of the Colorado Plateau—exceed fourteen thousand feet.

But perhaps the ultimate irony of this desert land is that not it raking winds, but water, has most shaped it. From the angry summer cloudbursts—"male rains," the Navajos call them—to the soft rains of autumn, the "female rains," water has been pervasive in its influence over this land.

As the plateau buckled upward, water flowed more powerfully and the land's surface warped and cracked, allowing the forces of water erosion to intensify.

This erosion was further hastened by the lack of vegetation to slow the water and impede its ability to gouge into the land. The Sierra Nevada, the towering mountains of eastern California and western Nevada, block the flow of moisture inland from the Pacific, creating a desert upon the Colorado Plateau.

The resulting cataclysmic erosion has peeled open the layers of time represented by the rock sediments of the Colorado Plateau, shaping some of the planet's most spectacular canyons and exposing long-buried geologic formations. This has freed the relics of the ages, leaving fossils, the bones of huge dinosaurs, and petrified forests from the primordial past strewn across the landscape as though tossed there by a giant at play.

It has also created a land unique in color.

Like nowhere else on Earth, this is a land of vividly colored rock—red, brown, chocolate, orange, roan, lavender, and a hundred shades between—each color and each layer conceived in a different geologic epoch, one color perhaps the remains of a petrified sand dune, another the mud from a long-forgotten lake, another a last remnant of some primordial river.

ANGEL ARCH, MOLAR ROCK, CANYONLANDS NATIONAL PARK, UTAH

YAVAPAI POINT, SOUTH RIM, GRAND CANYON NATIONAL PARK, ARIZONA

Grand Canyon - Staircase into Time

If an eagle were to soar above the South Rim of Arizona's Grand Canyon—assuming it was a clear day without smog invading the canyon from distant Southern California or from the coal-fired Mohave Generating Station in Laughlin, Nevada—spread out below and for as far as the great raptor could see to the north would be the nearest thing to a time machine to be found on Earth.

From the bottom of the Grand Canyon more than a mile below to its rim and spread out as a series of cliffs across the distant northwest horizon is a vista representing nearly two billion years of geology—the Grand Staircase.

Here, the cataclysmic erosion that has torn into the Colorado Plateau has created a staircase into the remote past, a place where it is possible to look at cross sections of vast accumulations of earth and stone and see a chronology—from bottom to top, past to present—of hundreds of millions of years of Earth's natural history.

Geologists have divided that history into four eras, marked by usually unexplained mass extinctions at the end of each and by a proliferation of new life at the dawning of the new:

• The Precambrian, dating from the Earth's beginning 4.6 billion years ago to 570 million years ago—eighty-five percent of Earth's history—was a time when the planet slowly became populated with the first multicellular life.

•The Paleozoic, from 570 million years ago to 245 million years ago, was the Age of Oceans and of invertebrates, including millipedes and scorpions. First came, snails, clams, and corals, followed by fish, amphibians, and reptiles.

• The Mesozoic, from 245 million years ago to 65

10

million years ago, was the Age of Dinosaurs.

• The Cenozoic—the present era—is the Age of Mammals.

The Grand Staircase—as revealed at Grand, Zion and Bryce canyons and elsewhere on the Colorado Plateau—offers a record in rocks, soil, fossils, and dinosaur bones from parts of all those eras.

When the current, massive erosional episode began a recent five to ten million years ago, it tore into soil accumulations more than two miles deep that had been deposited upon the Colorado Plateau craton through long ages, and in places rapidly removed more than a mile of rock.

One such place is at the Grand Canyon, where more than a mile of rocks and soil are already gone from *above* the rim of the canyon!

The remaining erosion-ravaged vista is a view into times predating, by hundreds of million of years, the Age of Dinosaurs!

The mighty Colorado River has cut sharply downward through the remaining mile-thick Grand Canyon rock layers, in the process carving the most spectacular canyon on Earth—one of the Seven Wonders of the World—and cutting so deeply into the land that it penetrated the very basement rocks upon which the continental craton rests!

At Granite Gorge, in the depths of the Grand Canyon, Precambrian-era rocks—from the first geologic era of the planet—rest, black, craggy, and twisted, having been cut into down to a depth of nearly fifteen hundred feet by the churning, persistent waters of the Colorado. These ancient, grizzled granites, called *Visnu Schist*, may be close to two billion years old.

These rocks probably began as silt and sand at the bottom of one of the planet's early oceans and contain chemical evidence of early life—single-celled algae—which first came into being about 2.5 billion years ago.

Time plodded on and about 1.7 billion years ago, these then-sedimentary rocks, thousands of feet thick, were pushed deep into the earth by catastrophic tectonic forces produced as some primordial continent, moving across the planet's molten mantle, collided with what is now the Colorado Plateau. This gave birth to a gigantic mountain range, perhaps as large as today's Himalayas, themselves being formed as India plows into Asia.

The sedimentary rocks were pushed downward to become the roots of the long-ago mountains and to be warped, twisted, and changed—or metamorphosed—into dark, black granite by the crushing pressures and resulting heat.

Over hundreds of millions of years, this great mountain range was eroded away until only the deeply buried roots remained. The region then uplifted again—although not as extensively—about 1.3 billion years ago, to be eroded down again.

Beginning about a billion years ago, seas again covered the area and four distinct layers of limestone, sandstone, and shale—the Grand

LIPAN POINT, SOUTH RIM, GRAND CANYON

Canyon Series—were deposited on top of the remnants of the vanished mountain range, then were faulted and tipped at an angle by geologic upheavals and eroded nearly away.

This erosion cost the canyon a half-billion years of its record, a missing chunk of Grand Canyon geology known as the Great Unconformity.

The inner Grand Canyon is a narrow, deep gorge, about sixty feet wide at its narrowest, because the rocks, compressed for ages deep within the Earth, are hard and tremendously resistant to erosion. Even the raging power of the Colorado River carved a path only by its persistence and the tremendous abrasiveness of the rock, sand, and silt suspended in its turbulent waters.

Immediately above the deep, inner gorge of the canyon is evidence of the dawning of the

VISNU SCHIST, INNER GORGE

Cambrian Period of Paleozoic time—the Tonto Plateau—now an expansive yucca- and cactus-studded benchland resting far above the river.

The Tonto Plateau is formed of relatively hard—and erosion resistant—Tapeats Sandstone, probably deposited near the shore of a primordial ocean roughly 570 million years ago.

It was then that most land masses were dispersed across the Southern Hemisphere, with one large continent spread across the South Pole, and several much smaller continents— including what is now the Colorado Plateau—strung out along the equator.

From here upward, the canyon broadens precipitously, the product of softer overlying rocks that succumbed more readily to erosion.

Between the Tapeats and the canyon rim five thousand to seven thousand feet above, depending upon the part of the canyon, are twelve surviving rock layers—put down between 570 million and 240 million years ago—that reflect the Paleozoic, a time when life evolved from primitive to ever-more complex sea creatures, and then to the first amphibians crawling from the sea onto land.

Just above the Tapeats, another 90 million years of the geologic record—residues of the Ordovician and Silurean geologic periods of early Paleozoic times—were eroded away or for some reason were never deposited at the Grand Canyon, creating another unconformity. The remaining rock layers between this point and the rim form an otherwise more-or-less intact record of the Devonian, Mississippian, and Permian geologic periods of the Paleozoic.

Through these eras, the Colorado Plateau craton remained in a mostly stable position at or slightly south of the equator. That lack of movement spared the region the turmoil and seismic activity—mountain building, faulting, volcanism—that accompany continental drift activity. And with mostly flat terrain, there was little erosion to remove what the ages were building.

During the Paleozoic, the Grand Canyon region was a continental shelf—a boundary between a coastline and the sea—and experienced five episodes of being barely out of water or somewhat submerged as the coastline fluctuated.

It was during the waning few million years of the Paleozoic, about 245 million years ago, that the Pangean supercontinent conglomerated.

And close to the end of the Paleozoic, a broad, white band of rock—Kaibab Limestone—was deposited, eventually to profoundly shape the Grand Canyon.

This roughly three hundred foot-thick layer of whitish, gray rock—looking like a gigantic bathtub ring around the rim of the canyon—was deposited as the first amphibians crawled from the sea.

Here, and across surrounding expanses of the Colorado Plateau, limestone, dolomite, and chert—a material that would be used hundreds of millions of years later by Indians to make arrowheads and spear points—were deposited as sponges and other hard-shelled sea creatures died and sank to an ocean floor. The resulting accumulations of silica, under the later burden of the mile-thick overlying rock layers, was compressed into the Kaibab Formation.

Hundreds of millions of years later, this tough, unyielding formation resisted erosion and shielded the underlying rocks. Without it, much of the Grand Canyon would likely have eroded away to some far less dramatic or rugged canyon.

But then, the Paleozoic—the Age of Oceans—drew to a close, and along with it, the Grand Canyon's spectacular part in the chronology of this land.

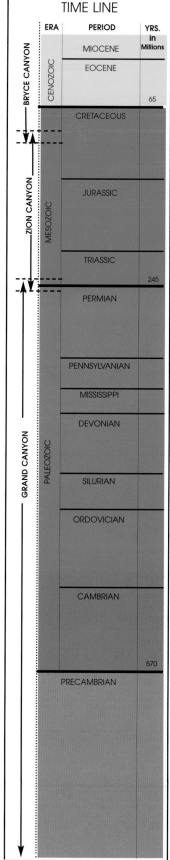

TIME LINE

ERA	PERIOD	YRS. in Millions
CENOZOIC	MIOCENE	
	EOCENE	
		65
MESOZOIC	CRETACEOUS	
	JURASSIC	
	TRIASSIC	
		245
PALEOZOIC	PERMIAN	
	PENNSYLVANIAN	
	MISSISSIPPI	
	DEVONIAN	
	SILURIAN	
	ORDOVICIAN	
	CAMBRIAN	
		570
	PRECAMBRIAN	

BRYCE CANYON

ZION CANYON

GRAND CANYON

The Colorado River

From the rim of the Grand Canyon far above, it may appear to be little more than a silvery ribbon threading its way through the canyon.

But in the great, imposing silence that often dominates the Grand Canyon, the mighty Colorado River can nonetheless still be heard, even from the rim thousands of feet above--a distant, unrelenting roar as the river persists in the task it began just a few million years ago: the carving of the Grand Canyon through the heart of the Kaibab Uplift, an enormous anticline spanning the Kaibab and Coconino Plateaus.

The Colorado has cut a mile-deep, ten-mile-wide chasm, so effectively dividing the huge anticline from east to west that animals on the North Rim of the Grand Canyon have evolved differently than those on the South Rim.

The Colorado River is not a large river by the standards of damper lands, but powerful as it flows from off the heights of the Rocky Mountains, the river's headwaters beginning in Rocky Mountain National Park in northern Colorado. The Colorado River then flows down the face of the continent toward the Gulf of California, 1,450 miles downstream, draining over 244,000 square miles and dropping over two vertical miles.

Meanwhile, the Green River, flows south from Wyoming into Utah to join the Colorado in Canyonlands National Park.

The Colorado then flows into the confines of Lake Powell, the two-hundred-mile-long reservoir with 1,950 miles of shoreline, created in 1963 by a giant concrete wedge of a dam at Page, Arizona.

The Colorado is one of the most dammed and diverted rivers on Earth, providing water for agriculture and cities--Las Vegas, Los Angeles, San Diego, Phoenix, Tucson--miles away from its natural course, or sometimes, as in the case of Denver and Albuquerque, on the other side of the Continental Divide. In fact, so much water is diverted from the Colorado, the river most years dries up long before it reaches the Gulf of California.

After Glen Canyon, an already significantly humbled and tamed Colorado River, by now joined by the San Juan River, flows from Lake Powell into the refuge of its age-old Grand Canyon.

There, between Lee's Ferry and Lake Mead 278 miles downstream, the Colorado drops an amazing nineteen hundred feet, a steep gradient that contributes significantly to the river's ability to cut into the depths of the Kaibab Uplift.

At one time, the Colorado was a huge, angry, roaring freight train of a river, carrying enormous accumulations of silt, gravel, and even boulders--an estimated average of 400,000 tons of detritus a day. But now, tamed by Glen Canyon Dam upstream--which is rapidly filling with sediments that settle out of the river--the Colorado River is much smaller and carries only about 80,000 tons of silt a day.

The Colorado is assisted in its daunting task of carving the Grand Canyon. As the river cuts downward, creating the depth of the canyon, small streams and rainwater flow toward the river from the sides, widening the canyon.

And the Colorado and other rivers, like the rest of this land, are affected by the Colorado Plateau's ocean heritage, picking up a burden of salt from ancient underground salt deposits. This happens as salt-laden springs flow into the river or its tributaries, as the rivers cut downward into salt deposits, or as agricultural irrigation runoff carrying fertilizer residues seeps into the ground or picks up natural salts before seeping back into the Colorado Plateau's rivers.

In the past, there was sufficient water in the Colorado to dilute the salt, but with each new water diversion, the salt concentrations increase, to the extent that the United States has built a desalination plant on the lower Colorado River in an attempt to at least partially clean up the river's brackish waters before they flow over the border into neighboring Mexico.

INNER GORGE, GRAND CANYON

AERIAL VIEW, ZION NATIONAL PARK, UTAH

Zion Canyon - The Middle Era

While "younger" soils a mile or more thick have eroded from above the rim of the Grand Canyon, they have survived elsewhere on the Colorado Plateau and contain recollections of tens of millions of years of the Pangean supercontinent and the world after Pangea fragmented, first into two huge continents, Gondwanaland on the south and Laurentia on the north, and then the continents we now know.

During these times, the Colorado Plateau moved from near the equator, north and west nearly two thousand miles, through nearly forty degrees of latitude and forty or fifty degrees of longitude.

The world that existed during the beginning of this the middle geologic era was a world dominated by dinosaurs.

On the distant northwest horizon of the Grand Canyon, beyond the ponderosa-pine carpeted Kaibab Plateau of the canyon's North Rim, can be seen a line of cliffs on the extreme western edge of the Colorado Plateau.

There, at the White Cliffs of Zion Canyon, is the most intact and dramatic record of the central part of the Grand Staircase and the planet's middle history, although Arches, Canyonlands, Petrified Forest and Capitol Reef national parks, Dinosaur National Monument, Glen Canyon

National Recreation Area and hundreds of places between also offer their own breathtaking glimpses into the Age of Dinosaurs.

That age began 245 million years ago and ended, probably with the K-T Impactor—a huge asteroid estimated to have been about five miles across—that slammed into Mexico's Yucatan Peninsula 65 million years ago. Many scientists believe this asteroid sent huge accumulations of debris high into the atmosphere that then rained back down, igniting forest fires across great swaths of the planet. The resulting dust and smoke shut out the sunlight, triggering the equivalent of a nuclear winter that killed most life on the planet by freezing or starvation.

All of these places on the Colorado Plateau hold, in sometimes unimaginable proliferation, evidence of the world as it was before that cataclysm: the bones and graveyards of dinosaurs; footprints of dinosaurs and vestiges of primordial forests where dinosaurs hunted, grazed, and were born and died; or simply reminders of lands and ecosystems that existed at the same time as the dinosaurs.

Zion National Park's particularly intact chronology of these times begins just beneath the floor of the astounding, steep-walled canyon. There rests the same Kaibab Limestone that caps the Grand Canyon. Above the Kaibab is stacked more than 2,500 feet of rock, a record of the Mesozoic and another 180 million years of Earth's geologic history.

And just as the Grand Canyon was cut into the surface of the Colorado Plateau by a river only in relatively recent geologic history, so too was Zion Canyon. But while the Grand Canyon was cut by the turbulent, churning waters of the Colorado, Zion was carved from solid rock by the Virgin River, usually—but not always—little more than a sparkling, playful stream.

Sometimes, with the downpours of summer monsoons, the Virgin River turns into a raging torrent, as water pours off surrounding immense expanses of rock to dump into the canyon with unfathomable force. But while many rivers carve canyons by eroding straight down into the surface of a relatively flat plain, the Virgin River flows off the west edge of the Kolob Terrace of Utah's Markagunt Plateau, in the process eroding back into the plateau like a knife cutting at an angle into the edge of a cake.

This means that upstream at the so-called Narrows, the Virgin River is cutting a narrow, forbidding slit, two thousand feet or more deep and often less than eighteen feet wide, while several miles downstream, an older but once-similar slit has been broadened by erosion to more than twelve hundred feet across.

And the journey of the Virgin River through solid rock has carved great stone edifices of nearly incomprehensible size and scale, sometimes towering more than a dizzying 2,600 feet high. Reflecting their effect on the human imagination, these bear names as epic and as dramatic as the land from which they were carved, names such as Angel's Landing, Altar of Sacrifice, Temple of Sinawava, Tabernacle Dome, Mountain of the Sun, and the Great White Throne.

And these rocks, like the walls of the Grand Canyon, bear a chronology of what this land has seen.

Just above the Kaibab Limestone, as it lies beneath the floor of Zion, are the chocolate brown-to-red soils of the Moenkopi Formation, water-origin deposits in places nearly eighteen hundred feet thick. These deposits were put down roughly 240 million years ago when this area was still a broad, shallow Pangean coastal plain that slowly became dry, probably as the sea receded or moved further west at the dawning of the Triassic.

Several million years later, water washed away the upper layers of the Moenkopi Formation and left behind the comparatively narrow two-hundred-foot-thick Shinarump Formation, made up of rocks and gravel washed across a hundred thousand square mile area, perhaps off a highlands or mountain range to the east in what is now Colorado and northern New Mexico.

ABOVE: GREAT WHITE THRONE, ZION CANYON

Then, 215 million years ago, a huge river found its way through the heart of what is now the near-center of the Colorado Plateau, flowing from north Texas, northwest to the sea in what is now Nevada. This broad tropical river—probably similar to the Amazon of our times—left huge deposits of river silts, shales, sandstone, and fresh-water limestone, the Chinle Formation, across much of the Southwest during the late Triassic.

The Chinle Formation has done much to shape—and color—northern Arizona, providing the reds, browns, pinks, purples, grays, maroons and whites of the Painted Desert, southeast of Zion Canyon in north-central Arizona near Holbrook and partially protected within the confines of Petrified Forest National Park.

VIRGIN RIVER, ZION CANYON

The deep, flowing waters of this great primordial river carried logs of giant dinosaur-era conifer trees—one hundred to two hundred feet high—downstream, where they caught in logjams and were buried under deep accumulations of mud, silt, and ash from volcanoes erupting to the south. Silicate and minerals in ground water infiltrated the cell structure of the huge logs, slowly turning wood to stone and creating the petrified wood of what we now call the Petrified Forest.

There, the primordial giants rested until the Colorado Plateau uplifted in the recent past, breaking and cracking the huge, petrified logs buried within its soils and loosing erosion to free them from where they had long been entombed.

And above the Chinle Formation at Zion Canyon were deposited, roughly 195 million years ago, the much shallower Moenave and Kayenta formations. Rivers still flowed through Zion, but smaller, humbler rivers, perhaps because the Colorado Plateau portion of a by-then fragmented Pangea had moved north into drier latitudes.

While dinosaur bones have not been found at Zion, the Kayenta Formation is rich in the tracks left as three-toed, upright-walking dinosaurs roamed over a flood plain at the edge of a desert.

Then, 190 million years ago in early Jurassic times, as North America moved further north into even drier regions, life grew scarcer at Zion as it was smothered by the dunes of a relentless Sahara-like desert, probably at the edge of a sea. Tremendous accumulations of sand—in Zion, two thousand feet thick or more—slowly spread over 150,000 square miles of the Colorado Plateau, distant Wyoming and western Colorado, and eventually, under the weight of overlying rock layers, were compressed into Navajo Sandstone.

It is the solid, towering heights of Navajo Sandstone—upon which wind-drift patterns cut by long-ago winds can still be seen—that form much of the dramatic vertical walls of Zion Canyon and influence much of the rugged landscape of Arches, Canyonlands, and a dozen or more other national parks and monuments of the Colorado Plateau. Because of the depths of its accumulations and because the sandstone is hard enough to somewhat resist erosion, Navajo Sandstone forms some of the Colorado Plateau's most spectacular formations.

But then, about 170 million years ago, even the great desert began to fade as North America moved to damper climates well north of the equator.

During mid-Jurassic time, streams and shallow seas deposited layers of clay and silt on top of the Navajo Sandstone, but then a desert again moved briefly into the region, leaving behind a thin layer of sandstone—sediments known as the Temple Cap Formation.

Then, the area again grew damp and streams eroded part of what had been deposited in mid-Jurassic time. A sea to the west periodically moved in and out of the region, ultimately leaving behind the 850-foot-thick Carmel Formation, deposits rich in the fossils of marine creatures and, perhaps, evidence of nearby volcanos.

Finally, about 100 million years ago, after a period of erosion that removed all late-Jurassic records, Zion was again only slightly above sea level, as indicated by a rich collection of the fossils of land plants, clams, and other small sea creatures found in the Dakota Formation.

Zion Canyon's narrative of the Age of Dinosaurs ended then, as astounding changes and an era of geological violence came to the Colorado Plateau.

DINOSAURS!

About 145 million years ago, much of what is now Colorado, Utah, Wyoming, New Mexico, and Arizona was covered with swamps, lakes, rolling hills, and thick forests of ferns, ginkgo, and Araucarioxylon trees—towering, slender pine-like trees related to today's monkey-puzzle trees.

Living beneath these giants in the primeval world of late Pangean times were a dozen or more dinosaur species of every size and shape, ranging from some of the largest ever—Seismosaurus, Brontosaurus, Camarasaurus, and Brachiosaurus—to the tiny, foot-high Nano-saurus, and the vicious hunter, Allosaurus, and the spike-backed herbivore, Stegosaurus.

The region was relatively dry part of the year, but it also experienced heavy rains that caused floods and mud flows that swept any dinosaur corpses that happened to litter the landscape into rivers, often to accumulate on sandbars or in river bends. There, the corpses partially decomposed, then were buried in mud and sand, where minerals slowly entered and fossilized the bones' cell structure petrifying and preserving them.

QUARRY, DINOSAUR NATIONAL MONUMENT, UTAH

As time moved on, this layer—known as the Morrison Formation—was buried to an eventual depth of nearly a mile under volcanic ash, mud, and other sediments.

While the Morrison—deposited about halfway through the 160-million-year reign of the dinosaurs—is the only formation on the Colorado Plateau containing dinosaur bones, it is one of the richest caches in the world.

It was in the Morrison, eroding from the upper reaches of New Mexico's San Juan Basin, that the enormous dinosaur *Seismosaurus hallonum* and about thirty other dinosaurs were found entombed. Seismosaurus' remains were excavated in the late 1980s and removed to New Mexico's Museum of Natural History in Albuquerque.

Similarly, other types of super-sized dinosaurs—*Ultrasaurus macintoshi*, *Supersaurus viviani*, and *Dystylosuarus edwini*—were found in the Morrison Formation at the Dry Mesa Quarry just southeast of Delta, Colorado.

And it was at Morrison, Colorado—where the Morrison Formation was first identified—that in 1887 a treasure-trove of dinosaur bones was discovered, far to the east of the Colorado Plateau in a hogback at the boundary between the Great Plains and the Rocky Mountains. This miles-long ridge—stretching parallel to the Rockies—was bent upward about 65 million years ago during the Laramide orogeny, when deep Precambrian basement rocks were shoved skyward during the birth of the Rocky Mountains, violently snapping and bending adjoining rock layers.

Similar geologic processes exposed the Morrison Formation—and dinosaur bones—along the Uncompahgre Uplift at Colorado National Monument near Grand Junction, Colorado; in Rabbit Valley to the west of Grand Junction; and along the San Rafael Anticline's west flank, near Price, Utah.

But dinosaur bones were exposed most spectacularly at Dinosaur National Monument, along the extreme northern reaches of the Colorado Plateau.

There, forces that about 65 million years ago uplifted the Uintah Mountains in northern Utah—the only mountain range in the mountain West to run east to west—also created the Split Mountain Anticline, near the Utah-Colorado border. There, the Morrison and other rocks were tipped to a roughly seventy-five-degree angle, setting into play rapid erosion that soon began freeing the formation's hoard from the Age of Dinosaurs—fossilized bones discovered by scientist Earl Douglass in 1909 and subsequently excavated for the Carnegie Museum in Pittsburgh, Pennsylvania.

In 1915, the site was protected within the boundaries of Dinosaur National Monument, and a building was eventually constructed to cover the quarry—one of the most studied and visited dinosaur sites in the world. Within, over two thousand bones remain exposed to view, although other Jurassic-vintage bones rest elsewhere in the monument.

It is within the Jackpile Sandstone member of the Morrison, meanwhile, that much of the uranium that brought a Cold War-era mining boom to the Colorado Plateau is found, especially along the southern reaches of the San Juan Basin, near Grants, New Mexico, and at Laguna Pueblo. The "yellow cake" formed as uranium-bearing ground water percolated into buried plant debris, where the uranium was caught and retained.

The Highlands - The Recent Past

In the blinding light of a summer day, the ghostly spires—called hoodoos—at Bryce Canyon National Park seem to radiate with an inner light, a strange iridescence that changes shade, even color, with the movement of the sun across the sky.

Or, there is the haunting beauty after an autumn storm, as fog shrouds this south-central Utah highland—the top of the Grand Staircase. The eerie forms seem to float out of nowhere to stand ethereal and unreal before again disappearing into the fog.

These strange rock formations on the nine thousand foot Paunsaugunt Plateau and, to a lesser degree, to the northwest on the nearby ten thousand foot Markagunt Plateau, and the soils immediately beneath them, reflect roughly 100 million years of Earth's relatively recent geologic history—from a time when new life was coming to the planet after the extinction of the dinosaurs.

While reflecting, from a human perspective, unfathomably long ages, even the oldest soils at Bryce Canyon—actually not a canyon at all, but a series of fourteen amphitheaters etched into the side of the Paunsaugunt Plateau by erosion—and nearby Cedar Breaks National Monument represent geologic times more easily understood than those at Zion and Grand canyons.

Bryce Canyon and Cedar Breaks are not so obscured in the remote past, and they are part of a world that, by 80 million to 65 million years ago, was gaining familiar features and life.

But during these times, the orderly, relatively logical accumulations, one era overlying another, that had persisted for hundreds of millions of years, came to an abrupt and violent end.

The dawning of Tertiary period of the early Cenozoic saw tumultuous folding, faulting, volcanism, and mountain building unparalleled on the Colorado Plateau since Precambrian time. After hundreds of millions of years of logical sedimentation in a region at or slightly above sea level, colossal tectonic forces moved across the western United States, giving birth over 40 million years to huge mountain ranges, and faulting and fracturing the Great Basin to the west and northwest of the Colorado Plateau.

This tumult, called the Laramide orogeny, was probably triggered as the westward-moving North American continental plate collided with the Pacific oceanic plate, causing it to begin slipping beneath North America. This created pressures deep underground that buckled the central regions of the continent upward into mountain ranges, forced magma from the Earth's molten mantle twenty miles or more underground to the surface to give birth to volcanos, and caused a roughly circular portion of the continental craton—now the Colorado Plateau—to rotate slightly.

First, the mighty Sierra Nevada were shoved skyward in California, and then, the Rocky Mountains from Canada deep into New Mexico. During only the last two million years or so, these mountains were further carved into jagged spires by multiple episodes of recent Pleistocene glaciation.

About 65 million years ago, fairly late in the Laramide orogeny, came the birth of southwestern Colorado's mighty San Juan Mountains, the state's youngest and, therefore, most rugged peaks.

The nearly incomprehensible might of these tectonic forces is perhaps best illustrated in the colossal pinnacles of the Needle Mountains in the Weminuche Wilderness north of Durango, Colorado. There, dark, twisted Precambrian granites—similar to those at the bottom of the Grand Canyon and also once deep basement rocks—

CEDAR BREAKS NATIONAL MONUMENT, UTAH

PREVIOUS PAGE, BRYCE CANYON NATIONAL PARK, UTAH

were shoved skyward to over fourteen thousand feet above sea level!

Elsewhere in the San Juans—in the dark, sinister Uncompahgre Canyon south of Ouray and in the jagged Grenadier Range south of Silverton—tectonic forces tilted huge blocks of Precambrian granite on end to form cliffs or peaks thousands of feet high.

One of the Southwest's most spectacular canyons, the Black Canyon of the Gunnison—immediately to the north of the San Juans—was also carved from ancient, ancient rocks. There, an enormous block of Precambrian granite was uplifted about 60 million years ago, to be buried about 25 million years later by ash spewing from volcanos in the San Juans and to the north, in the Elk Mountains.

These ash accumulations diverted the Gunnison River, forcing it to flow—in its journey west and then north toward the Colorado River—directly across the surface of the what is now known as the Gunnison Uplift.

The Gunnison is a powerful little river due to the 2,100 feet it drops in only fifty miles and the abrasive silt, rocks, even boulders, it carries in its churning waters. Over the last few million years, the Gunnison has sliced a forbidding, sheer-walled canyon over two thousand feet into solid granite, and at the Black Canyon's 2,250 foot-high Painted Wall, created Colorado's highest cliff.

And to the east of the San Juans, just beyond the boundaries of the Colorado Plateau, sands eroded from off the towering mountains have created their own legacy: the continent's highest sand dunes.

BRYCE AMPHITHEATER

For century after century, millennia after millennia, prevailing winds from the southwest swept the sands accumulated on the floor of the great San Luis Valley northeastward to the base of the Sangre de Cristo Mountains, until dunes over seven hundred feet high—now Great Sand Dunes National Monument—rested at the base of the Sangre de Cristos.

And just as the logical downward erosion at the Grand and other canyons of the Colorado Plateau exposed great ages of rocks and soils for our times to see, so too did the turmoil in the San Juans. In the Animas River Valley between Silverton, Colorado, and the New Mexico border, for example, rocks from all four geologic eras—Precambrian, Paleozoic, Mesozoic, and Cenozoic—once resting in logical layers deep within the Earth are revealed in now-jumbled order in a turmoil-twisted terrain.

But long before the massive mountain-building era, the Dakota Formation—the same rock layer that tops Zion Canyon—was put down about 100 million years ago in a shallow sea at what is now Bryce Canyon. Above this layer rests blue-gray Mancos Shale, the remains of a vast inland sea that 90 to 80 million years ago stretched from the Gulf of Mexico to the Arctic Circle, followed by residues—Mesaverde Sandstone—left as the sea retreated.

And as the mountains rose in the west, blocking out the seas that had for so long rested there, the lands between the Rocky Mountains and the Sierra Nevada subsided into gigantic basins.

It was in one of these, about 60 million years ago, that a huge fresh-water lake, Lake Flagstaff, stretched for over two hundred miles from Salt Lake City into south-central Utah. There, through millions of years, sediments accumulated to eventual depths of more than two thousand feet.

Finally, when the Colorado Plateau uplifted in the relatively recent past, several great blocks of deep, underground rock in south-central Utah—today's Paunsaugunt, Markagunt, Sevier, Awapa, Wasatch, Gunnison, and Aquarius plateaus—were faulted upward.

At the Paunsaugunt and Markagunt plateaus, the ancient lake bed sediments—radically raised and tilted by the faulting—were exposed to rapid erosion that carved spectacular amphitheaters into the plateaus' sides. These amphitheaters are filled with hauntingly beautiful badlands, hoodoos, and some of the most rugged terrain on Earth.

Left behind in these long-ago sediments of Lake Flagstaff are deposits of iron, calcium carbonate, manganese oxide, and limonite, which have stained and colored the hoodoos and badlands, causing them sometimes to seem to glow and change colors with the progression of the day.

SMALL WORLDS

The Colorado Plateau is a land of enormous size, of vast, unoccupied distances stretching beyond the rim of remote horizons. But it is also a place of small worlds, the life in which has survived in their own tiny niches since long before the dinosaurs.

On the benchlands of the Grand Canyon and Canyonlands national park, in Arches and Capitol Reef national parks—anywhere there are great expanses of rock, especially Navajo Sandstone, that has many indentions in which water can pool—there are so-called potholes, natural cisterns where water accumulates, each unique, a world unto itself.

A pothole—or if it is large, a t a n k — c a n remain bone dry for years, empty of water and all signs of life, except perhaps lichen growing at its edge. But then, with the arrival of rain to fill these natural basins, life bursts forth in a race against the clock and the baking heat.

Almost magically, the life-forms appear, with names appropriate to their e p h e m e r a l nature, fairy shrimp, ghost, seed, and tadpole shrimp, living in the company of gnats, snails, tadpoles, and other tiny aquatic creatures.

They have only a few short weeks to finish their entire life cycle and leave behind eggs buried in pothole-bottom sands to renew life when the rain finally comes again. Or, others among them, such as snails, pull back into the sanctuary of their shells and simply go dormant.

The eggs of the shrimp—some of them descendents of the long-extinct trilobites that lived in Cambrian ocean sediments—may survive a decade or more in a dry pothole. The tadpole shrimp species, meanwhile, may have existed in Pangean times, 245 million years ago.

Once hatched, the tiny creatures feed on algae, dirt, and organic matter blown into their pothole.

But while the wind can blow their eggs for miles, where they may land and help populate a new pothole, scientists have discovered each pothole to be unique and, often, biologically significantly different than all others, even nearby potholes.

But despite their ability to lie dried out and dormant for months or years, these pools are fragile and can fall easy victim to chemical contamination as simple as sunscreen washed from the body of a hiker bathing in a pothole's cool waters. Likewise, too many people replenishing water bottles or dipping water from the tiny oases can hasten the speed with which they dry out, reducing the chances for the critters they support to survive or have time to reproduce.

And there are the living soils— "brown sugar"— of the desert.

Especially in the piñon and juniper woodlands of the Colorado Plateau, the ground often looks black and spongy, in fact, a conglomeration of lichen, mosses, algae,

EL MALPAIS NATIONAL MONUMENT, NEW MEXICO

and fungi forming living colonies on the ground surface.

This fragile living crust, called cryptogamic soils, helps slow erosion, retain moisture, and provide a nurturing place for seeds to sprout.

Yet, though able to withstand blistering heat, wind, drought, and pounding rain, cryptogamic soil can be easily and fatally crushed, falling victim to something as simple as the footfall of a hiker or the tires of a bike ridden off established paths. Once crushed, it can take decades for cryptogamic soil to heal.

Salt and the Moving Earth

Probably because of the great thickness of its rock layers, the Colorado Plateau was spared much of—but not all—the violence that formed the Rocky Mountains and the Sierra Nevada. But the forces giving rise to the great mountain ranges were so profound, waves of the turmoil rippled far out across the Colorado Plateau.

Just as a sheet of metal pushed from both ends will bend toward the middle, so too did parts the Colorado Plateau buckle under pressures put upon it during the Laramide orogeny, especially as the towering San Juan Mountains of southwest Colorado began forcing their way skyward about 65 million years ago.

These colossal forces caused geologic faults, or fractures, which probably already existed, in the basement rocks deep within the Earth to slip vertically, bending and snapping overlying rock layers upward to form what are known as anticlines.

In their early years, the anticlines were probably relatively gentle, dome-like, elongated hills winding from north-to-south across miles of the Colorado Plateau, like giant ocean waves caught in mid-swell. But in the millions of years since their formation, erosion has removed much of the anticline's fractured and broken debris, leaving dramatically tilted rocks, or flatirons, exposed along the anticlines' sides.

The most extraordinary anticlines on the Colorado Plateau are the San Rafael Swell, the Waterpocket Fold, and the Comb Ridge, or Monument, Anticline.

The San Rafael Anticline is a sixty-five mile long, oval-shaped formation stretching northeast from near Hanksville to Cedar Mountain, Utah.

On the higher east side of the anticline is a spectacular barrier of jagged flatirons—the San Rafael Reef—tipped skyward at a dramatic angle toward the northwest and made up of rocks from the middle era of Earth history, the same vintage as those at Zion Canyon. But nearer the center is much older Kaibab Limestone, the same formation lining the rim of the Grand Canyon.

The rocks on the outside edge of the flatirons, originally on the surface of the ground, are younger, while those toward the bottom—and deeper, before the ground buckled—are older.

And to the south of the San Rafael Anticline is

the spectacular Waterpocket Fold of Capitol Reef National Park, stretching southeast for nearly one hundred miles from Thousand Lake Mountain in south-central Utah to the Colorado River near the Arizona border.

Capitol Reef—so named by early Mormon settlers because, like an ocean reef, it was a barrier to travel—is part of the greater Waterpocket Fold,

WATERPOCKET FOLD, UTAH

with its spectacular west-facing flatirons.

The rock layers warped skyward at a sharp angle along the Waterpocket Fold—named for pockets in the formation's Navajo Sandstone that catch and hold rain water—are also from the planet's middle geologic era, again with Kaibab Limestone just below the surface.

Finally, there is the eighty-five to ninety mile long Comb Ridge. The jagged flatirons of Comb Ridge begin near Blanding, Utah, head south along the eastern boundary of Monument Valley, and finally, swing southwest toward Kayenta, Arizona.

PREVIOUS PAGE: WHITE RIM SANDSTONE, CANYONLANDS NATIONAL PARK, UTAH

But it is the central eroded regions of this enormous anticline that have created a world-famous landscape: the towering bluffs, buttes, and pinnacles of Monument Valley.

Great accumulations of rocks from the Pennsylvanian and Permian periods of the Paleozoic—the same vintage as many of the rocks in the Grand Canyon—began

MONUMENT ANTICLINE

beneath oceans. Over roughly 30 million years, sea water flowed into the basin and back out, twenty-nine times in all. Each episode left behind sea water that evaporated. When the sea finally departed for the last time in late Pennsylvanian time, a mile-thick layer of salt, several types of minerals, and other residues were left behind. At the same

eroding from the anticline's heights when it uplifted about 65 million years ago, a process that first carved great mesas and then, from the mesas, the pinnacles, spires, and buttes that today form Monument Valley's dramatic landscape.

Meanwhile, still in antiquity, the San Juan River, flowing south out of the San Juan Mountains and then west across the desert, reached a depressed fault zone along the northern boundaries of the Monument Anticline and formed a lake where tens of millions of years of sediments accumulated to depths of hundreds of feet.

But when the Colorado Plateau uplifted during the last few million years, the Monument Valley region rose, draining the lake and leaving the San Juan River to cut downward through the lake sediments—in a confused, winding sort of way—creating in the process the deep, meandering oxbows of the Goosenecks of the San Juan.

But another element—salt—profoundly shaped the face of Colorado Plateau and helped create the rock legacy that today makes up Arches and Canyonlands national parks.

For reasons not clearly understood, about 300 million years ago in early Pennsylvanian time of the Paleozoic—55 million years or so before the continents conglomerated into Pangea—the region around Moab, Utah, subsided into a roughly eleven-thousand-square-mile, oval-shaped depression. This, the Paradox Basin, stretched from near today's Cortez in southwest Colorado, to just beyond Green River, in east-central Utah.

Meanwhile, a primordial mountain range—the Uncompahgre Uplift—rose immediately to the northeast, in extreme west-central Colorado and eastern Utah, probably when North and South America collided about 295 million years ago.

The Paradox Basin, like the rest of the Colorado Plateau, was a land repeatedly submerged

time, sediments from the eroding Uncompahgre Uplift were burying the salt residues, creating pressures that caused the salt to liquify and flow slowly to the southwest, where it finally encountered underground faults that diverted it upward into overlying rocks where it formed salt domes two to three miles high. This bowed overlying rock layers, creating enormous, domed anticlines throughout the Moab region, including the Salt Valley Anticline at Arches National Park.

This pressure also fractured overlying, brittle formation of sedimentary rock, along parallel lines.

Of tidal flat, desert dune, and beach sand origin, Entrada Sandstone was deposited roughly 140 million years ago and is one of the reasons why arches proliferate near Moab, but not elsewhere on the Colorado Plateau.

The Colorado Plateau's relatively recent erosional episode removed more than a mile of rock from above the Entrada. Once erosion exposed

CANYONLANDS NATIONAL PARK, UTAH

the Entrada Sandstone to the elements, weathering widened existing parallel fractures in the sandstone until they gradually created relatively narrow, free-standing formations, called fins. Such fins sometimes turned to arches—if the fin did not collapse during erosion—as underlying soft parts of the Entrada known as the Slick Rock Member, eroded away.

The result at Arches National Park is more than five hundred arches—the highest concentration in the world.

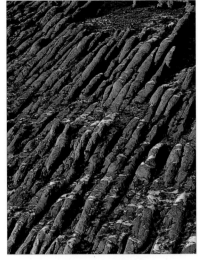

FINS FORMING, ENTRADA SANDSTONE

The same parallel fracturing—sometimes in combination with right-angled cracks—also created the region's often-checkerboarded expanses of sandstone and a topography of towers, spires, pinnacles and domes, especially at Arches and in the Needles and Maze districts of nearby Canyonlands National Park.

Natural bridges, as at Natural Bridges and Rainbow Bridge national monuments, are formed as a stream erodes through a sandstone block

Meanwhile, 80 miles to the northeast, near Grand Junction, Colorado, a 125 mile-long, 30 mile-wide block of Precambrian-era granite—again similar to that in the depths of the Grand Canyon—was uplifted during the last 65 million years into a huge anticline that today towers above the Grand Valley and the Colorado River.

The uplift, part of which is protected within the boundaries of Colorado National Monument, rests in the same region as the Uncompahgre Uplift of 300 million years ago. The uplift's granites were once the deep roots of the primordial mountain

range—but resting six thousand feet beneath their current position—while overlying sedimentary rocks were often warped and twisted by the uplifting process.

Another opportunity—in some ways nearly equal to that at the Grand Canyon—to look in awe at the landscapes of antiquity occurs at Canyonlands National Park.

Roughly 140 million years of geologic history have already been eroded away from above the rim of Canyonlands.

But Grand View Point in Canyonland's northern Island in the Sky District, overlooks bluffs, buttes, miles of twisted terrain, and the mighty Colorado and Green rivers, as they prepare to converge in the southern third of the park. That view is dramatically divided horizontally by a distinctive line of white rock resting about two-thirds of the way to the canyon bottom—a boundary between remote antiquity below and the somewhat more recent past above.

This White Rim Sandstone is made up of 245 million-year-old shallow coastal marine deposits and sand dunes—the same age and similar to the Kaibab Formation at the rim of the Grand Canyon. And like the Kaibab, the White Rim Sandstone is erosion resistant, forming a broad benchland above the narrower inner canyons of the Green and Colorado below.

In those inner canyons are formations of the

THE WINDOWS, ARCHES NATIONAL PARK, UTAH

same age as those in the upper levels of the Grand Canyon; above the White Rim are many of the same rocks—Navajo and Kayenta sandstones, the Chinle Formation, the Shinarump Conglomerate, and the Moenkopi Formation—found at Zion Canyon, another spectacular panorama from the Age of Dinosaurs, and before.

SHIP ROCK, NAVAJO RESERVATION, NEW MEXICO

Upheavals and Turmoil

About the same time the mighty San Juan Mountains were rising skyward in southwestern Colorado 65 million years ago, the land to the south of the great mountains was subsiding, creating what is today the roughly 25,000 square mile San Juan Basin.

Stretching from extreme southern Colorado on the north to the San Mateo Mountains near Grants, New Mexico, on the south, to the Chuska and Carrizo mountains in Arizona in the west, and to New Mexico's Nacimiento and Jemez mountains in the east, this gigantic basin, like the rest of the Colorado Plateau, was largely spared the violence of mountain-building forces.

Instead, it carries the bathtub-ring markings of primordial seas, vast badlands, and the graves of dinosaurs—including that near San Ysidro, New Mexico, of *Seismosaurus hallorum*, the longest dinosaur ever found, as its name implies, a literally earth-shaking dinosaur equal in length to three eighteen-wheel trucks parked end-to-end.

During the Laramide orogeny and subsequent ages, swarms of volcanos erupted across the Southwest from the Sierra Nevada to the Rocky Mountains.

Probably due to the thickness of its rock layers—which may have prevented magma from penetrating the surface—the Colorado Plateau saw comparatively few eruptions. But a ring of fire encircled the plateau at Mount Taylor in New

ANASAZI CAVE KIVA IN TUFF,
BANDELIER NATIONAL MONUMENT, NEW MEXICO

Mexico's San Mateo Mountains; along Arizona's Mogollon Rim to the south; near Saint George, Utah, on the west; and along northern Utah's Wasatch Front.

And volcanism did occasionally intrude onto the Colorado Plateau, at Zion and Bryce canyon, in the Grand Canyon, and north of Flagstaff, Arizona, at the San Francisco Peaks and at nearby Sunset Crater National Monument.

Enormous eruptions also occurred in the San Juan Mountains—fifteen or more stupendous eruptions—about 35 million years ago. The resulting ash accumulated to form some of the San Juan's most rugged peaks, especially in the Uncompahgre and Wilson ranges along the San Juan's northwest ramparts.

These eruptions brought base elements—including gold and silver—from deep within the Earth and injected them into the depths of the young mountains, sowing the seeds, to germinate some 35 million years later, for the mining boom of the 1880s and 1890s.

About the same time, especially violent eruptions broke through spectacularly and dramatically in the San Juan Basin and in northeast Arizona, in and near Monument Valley.

In these eruptions, superheated steam—caused when magma hits groundwater—exploded skyward, shattering the surface of the ground and sending a chaos of magma, once-deep granites, and sedimentary surface and near-surface rock—sometimes the size of cars—far into the air, to fall back into the hole created by the blast.

After these long-ago volcanos subsided and eventually became extinct, the ages eroded away the softer soils and rocks that formed the exterior cones, leaving behind only the interior volcanic plugs—often a mixture of basalt and rock debris—and sometimes, associated sills and dikes, to tower spectacularly up out of the flatness of the desert.

Several dozen of these structures, called diatremes, stand upon the Colorado Plateau, but perhaps most dramatically at Cabezon Peak in the south San Juan Basin, also west of San Ysidro, and at several locations near Kayenta, Arizona.

But by far the most spectacular diatreme is Ship Rock, a few miles southwest of the little town of Shiprock, New Mexico—Tsé Bit'ái', the "Rock With Wings", as the Navajos call it. Protruding out of the flatness of the San Juan Basin like a sailing ship at sea, Ship Rock towers 1,728 feet high—twenty stories higher than the World Trade Center.

Some thirty million years later, an even more catastrophic eruption happened along the eastern boundary of the Colorado Plateau, at the Rio Grande Rift in north-central New Mexico.

Often a deep, narrow chasm through which the Rio Grande flows in its journey from the San Juan Mountains to the Gulf of Mexico, this rift valley is, like Africa's Great Rift Valley, a place where the continent is literally tearing apart under tectonic pressures caused as the Pacific oceanic plate moves northward, brushing against the California coast and the western edges of the continent. Within another few million years, North America likely will have torn apart sufficiently for the Gulf of Mexico to flood into central New Mexico.

One of the few rivers in the Southwest that did not carve its own route to the sea, the Rio Grande merely chose to flow along the channel created by the rift.

As a testament to the forces at work, at Albuquerque, New Mexico, the west side of the rift, beginning about 30 million years ago, dropped some 20,000 feet, while the east side faulted upward 5,000 feet—creating the Sandia Mountains and a spectacular displacement of the surface, now largely filled with sediments, of at least 25,000 feet!

Volcanos periodically have erupted along this rift valley in recent geologic history, but none as spectacularly as the Jemez Volcano in the south Jemez Mountains.

The volcanic mountain towered many thousands of feet above the surrounding New Mexico landscape until the first of two great explosions, one 1.4 million and another 1.2 million years ago.

Each of these was hundreds of times more powerful than the 1980 eruption at Mount Saint Helens. The eruptions blew most of the enormous mountain to smithereens, rained rocks and debris down on distant Iowa, Nebraska, and Texas, and triggered lava flows that roared down the mountain at speeds probably approaching one hundred miles an hour.

The superheated ash compacted and fused together to form volcanic tuff cliffs hundreds of feet high, into which the Anasazi Indians over a million years later carved beehive-type dwellings at what is today Bandelier National Monument. And the resulting enormous accumulations of ash and pumice created the rugged Pajarito Plateau, along the east side of the Jemez Mountains, upon which Los Alamos—where the first atomic bombs were built during World War II—and Los Alamos National Laboratory now stand.

Left in the wake of the eruption was the Valles Caldera, at sixteen miles across one of the world's largest calderas.

Then, there were the laccoliths, volcanos that tried but could not penetrate the Colorado Plateau.

As magma pushed upward from deep within the Earth, it encountered the Colorado Plateau's thick crustal plate and overlying accumulations of sedimentary rock. Unable to break through to the surface, the resulting vertical columns of magma instead flowed out horizontally underground along weaknesses between the rock layers, often causing overlying sedimentary rocks to bulge upward thousands of feet higher than the surrounding terrain.

It was such unborn volcanos that created many of the Colorado Plateaus mountain ranges: the La Sals, along the Colorado-Utah border, the Henry and Abajo mountains of southeast Utah, the Carrizo Mountains in extreme northeast Arizona, and Navajo Mountain near the shores of Lake Powell in extreme southern Utah.

Notable among the laccoliths is Sleeping Ute Mountain, towering above southwest Colorado's Montezuma Valley, more-or-less parallel to the Utah border. Especially when viewed from immediately to the east at nearby Mesa Verde, the Sleeping Ute looks like a giant figure in repose, his arms folded over his chest.

Ute legend says this giant will some day arise from his slumber and banish whites from this land.

To the northeast, the Rico and La Plata ranges in the west San Juan Mountains are also laccoliths, while some geologists theorize that the Colorado Plateau itself may be a form of giant laccolith pushed higher than surrounding lands by the pressure of magma beneath.

In the desert, laccoliths, often ten thousand to twelve thousand feet high, are cool, damp oases above the brutal summer heat of the rock-dominated land at their feet.

Carpeted at their higher elevations with thick growths of aspen, Douglas fir, ponderosa pines, and furtile alpine meadows filled with lush grasses and flowers, many laccoliths rise above timberline, where their rugged peaks—usually made up of sedimentary rocks that once rested level with similar rocks on the desert floor—often are capped with snow.

The forests on these and other desert mountains are in and of themselves miraculous, perhaps the last surviving remnants of ice age forests—and perhaps much older—that once flourished across much of the continent, and even into what is today the arid Southwest and deep into Mexico.

As the land warmed, the moisture-loving plants moved northward on the continent, and regionally, moved up the mountains, finding sanctuary at high altitudes.

But scientists warn that global warming will quickly drive these isolated laccolith ecosystems

LA SAL MOUNTAINS, UTAH

to even higher elevations, sometimes forcing them, and the many rare plants and animals they contain, off the top of the mountains—and into oblivion. In the relatively near future, these cool, damp oases may be only a memory.

IMPACT!

In a place so old and so devoid of vegetation, it is perhaps inevitable that the Colorado Plateau bears so many visible, often dramatic, scars.

One such place is northern Arizona's Meteor Crater, the best-preserved and first-proven impact crater on Earth.

Another is Canyonlands National Park's mysterious Upheaval Dome.

About 50,000 years ago, a meteor weighing several hundred thousand tons slammed out of the northeastern sky at over thirty thousand miles an hour and plowed into the ground a few miles west of what is now Winslow, Arizona.

It struck with an explosive force greater than twenty million tons of TNT, a "yield" thousands of times greater than that of the first atomic bomb-

METEOR CRATER, ARIZONA

-estimated at twenty thousand tons of TNT--dropped on Japan in 1945.

As the meteor--at about 150 feet across, a fraction the size of the five-mile-wide K-T Impactor that may have caused the extinction of the dinosaurs--plowed through the atmosphere, it created shock waves that killed animals and caused devastation for miles around. And, as it slammed into the ground, the meteor vaporized rocks close to the impact area, shattered those further away, and squeezed chunks of graphite into tiny diamonds.

When the dust finally settled, a crater seven hundred feet deep and four thousand feet across smoldered where hours earlier there had been nothing but a broad, flat plain. Scientists attribute the crater's huge size to the speed of the meteor's impact--an impact which cast blocks

of limestone the size of houses onto the crater's rim and threw hundreds of tons of limestone, sandstone, and other debris a mile or more beyond the crater's rim.

Erosion and sedimentation have decreased the depth of Meteor Crater to about 550 feet--still deep enough to hold a sixty-story building.

In 1960, the Meteor Crater was conclusively identified as an impact crater by Dr. Eugene Shoemaker, then with the United States Geological Survey, and since known, along with his wife, Caroline, and another astronomer, for predicting the multiple impacts of fragments of Comet Shoemaker-Levy with Jupiter in 1994.

Meanwhile, at Canyonland's Upheaval Dome in Utah, scientists are still grappling with whether this bizarre formation in the Island in the Sky District was caused by an impact or was formed when a salt dome collapsed.

Because of little evidence of "ejecta"--rubble thrown about by an impact--or of instantaneous deformation of the area, some scientists are leaning toward the belief that Upheaval Dome, which resembles a mile-wide volcanic crater without lava, is a collapsed salt dome.

The dome likely formed when sea-origin salt from the Paradox Formation underlying Arches and Canyonlands national parks liquified and moved underground as the result of the weight of overlying rock layers and then was forced into weak places in overlying sediments, buckling them upward into a dome. This dome may have later collapsed into a crater as the salt flowed back out.

UPHEAVAL DOME, CANYONLANDS NATIONAL PARK, UTAH

THE INDIANS

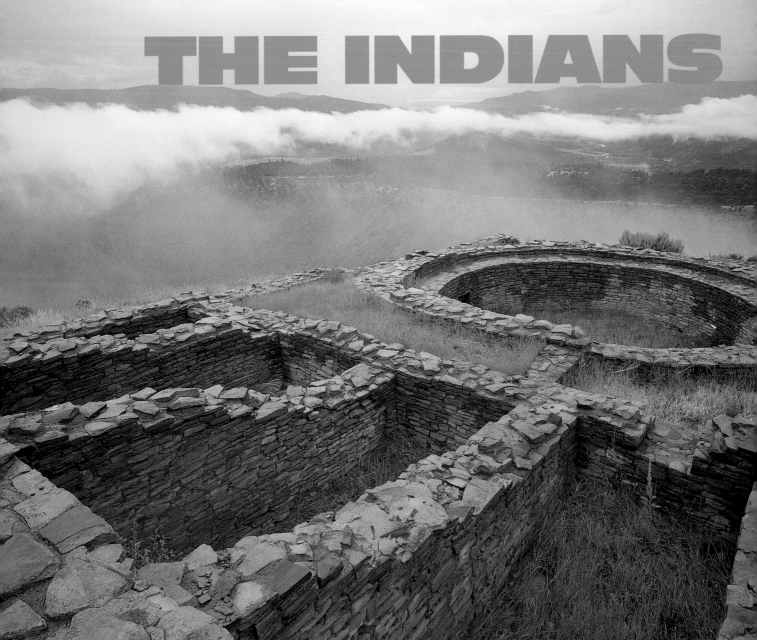

CHACO OUTLIER, ANASAZI CULTURE, CHIMNEY ROCK, COLORADO

The Ancients

They can be seen to the east of the highway between Bernalillo and Cuba, New Mexico, the centuries-old walls of Zia and Santa pueblos molded onto the face of the land over hundreds of years.

And in the shadow of the desert bluffs of the San Juan Basin, Monument Valley, the Painted Desert, and many places between can still be seen the rounded, conical shaped hogans of the Navajos, inevitably facing east toward the rising sun and almost as inevitably bordered by corrals holding sheep or horses. But in the new reality of a dawning millennium, the hogans often are also surrounded by mobile homes, prefab houses, or other buildings of our times.

And sometimes, along the banks of the Pine, Animas, Florida, Piedra, Navajo and other rivers of southwest Colorado or extreme northern New Mexico can be glimpsed an occasional tepee, usually with a car or two parked outside, of a Ute or Jicarilla Apache—at least some of whom try to embrace tradition in a rapidly changing Southwest.

Some Indians of the Colorado Plateau have lived in this colorful and beautiful land for thousands of years. Others have lived here not much longer than the European settlers.

And like the early European settlers, they are

PREVIOUS PAGES: THE THREE SISTERS, MONUMENT VALLEY NAVAJO TRIBAL PARK, ARIZONA-UTAH people of often diverse cultures, religions, and languages.

The term, "Indian" in fact refers to dozens upon dozens of different tribes and language groups—more than 250 in the United States and Canada. On the Colorado Plateau, the term refers to a half dozen or so tribes, people who may now share the common bond of speaking English, but whose native tongues or cultural roots are often as radically different as those of the French from the Japanese or the Germans from Russians.

Some of these present-day people include the Utes, who originally lived in the Colorado Plateau's rugged mountain region; the Pai, who long ago ventured into

BARRIER CANYON-STYLE PICTOGRAPHS, UTAH

the time-molded depths of the Grand Canyon; and the Southern Paiutes, who lived in southwest Utah near Zion and Bryce canyons.

There are the descendents of the long-ago Anasazi, the Pueblos, whose beautiful earth-colored villages stand upon the desert mesas as they have for nearly a thousand years, although in our times often sporting a television antenna or an occasional satellite dish.

And there are the relative newcomers, the Navajos and the Jicarilla Apaches, once nomads traveling the Southwest and Great Plains and undoubtedly some of the planet's most adaptable and resilient people.

All are tribes that a century ago were facing the crisis of whether their very existence, and certainly their way of life, might be threatened with the arrival of the next onslaught of settlers. They still face variations of that challenge, as mushrooming cities, the demand for resources, and the encroachment of an industrialized, often troubled, culture threaten their land and their ways.

But to understand where these tribes may be going in the future, it is important to see where they have been in the past and how this magnificent land, and their love of it, has shaped their languages, their religions, their cultures—every fiber of their existence.

The Indians of the Colorado Plateau and many other American Indians were living in the Americas thousands of years before the European explorer Columbus "discovered" the New World in 1492.

When humankind actually arrived in the Western Hemisphere remains obscured among the secrets of remote antiquity. The earliest conclusively proven human habitations—those of the ancient Clovis people—date from around twelve thousand years ago, but some evidence indicates humankind may have been here seventeen thousand years, and perhaps as long as forty thousand years.

New—and highly controversial evidence—also indicates that European people, not Asian, might have arrived in the Americas first.

The most commonly accepted theory is that humankind arrived from Asia sometime toward the end of the Pleistocene glacial period, twelve thousand to thirty thousand years ago. That ice age, beginning about two million years ago, brought four major glacial advances which nearly covered Canada with ice.

During colder weather and the resulting ice advances, enormous amounts of sea water were locked into glaciers, causing the sea level to drop. This may have exposed a land bridge across the Bering Sea, over which people traveled from Asia toward the end of the final glacial advance of the Pleistocene Ice Age and the Wisconsin glaciation.

But a recently discovered skeleton with possible European features might indicate a migration by early Clovis man from France—by sea—about twelve thousand years ago. Tools of these ancient people—evidence of whom has been found throughout North and South America—some experts believe, are similar to tools of the Solutreans of France.

Theory has it that the Solutreans, who may have first settled in Florida, might have been killed or genetically assimilated by later-arriving people.

But the debate may be largely academic if research ultimately proves still another people arrived in the Americas earlier than either the Clovis or Solutreans.

The first known inhabitants of the Southwest, including the Colorado Plateau, were Paleo

Indians.

Hunters and gatherers, they followed the movement of animals, including the great beasts—cave bears, long-horned bison, mammoths, camels, horses, sloths, and mastodons.

However, between 8,000 B.C. and 10,000 B.C., a radical decline in precipitation associated with the end of the Wisconsin glaciation triggered a massive drought, especially in the Southwest. This, along with excessive hunting and possibly disease, led to the extinction of most of the big animals. As a result, the Paleo Indians followed surviving game animals east onto the more hospitable Great Plains. There, the Paleo Indian hunting tradition survived well into historical times.

The Paleo Indians were gradually replaced in the Southwest by people of what archeologists call the Desert Archaic culture of Mexico, California, and the basin regions of the American West. The Desert Archaic culture dominated the Southwest, including the Colorado Plateau, from 6,000 B.C. to about 1 A.D. From that culture, which hunted animals that had survived the Pleistocene extinctions and put greater emphasis on gathering plants, emerged many of the colorful indigenous cultures of today's Colorado Plateau.

The Desert Archaic peoples moved across the land in what anthropologists call the "seasonal round," an annual migration during which they followed larger animals such as deer and elk into the high country in summer and back into the lower valleys and desert in the autumn, killing large and small animals and harvesting wild fruits, berries, seeds, roots, grasses, and grains.

About four thousand years ago, a primitive form of pod corn, the ancestor to maize, was brought into the Southwest from Mexico, and the Desert Archaic people made a subtle but important cultural modification.

As they began their spring seasonal round, they planted corn—a plant then found exclusively in the Americas—in protected lower canyons and valleys. When they returned in the fall, they harvested whatever crop had been produced by the untended plants. Soon, they were also planting squash, and by about three thousand years ago, at least in the southern areas of the Southwest, beans.

What archeologists and anthropologists call the "sacred triad"—corn, beans, and squash—the mainstay of the Native American agriculture, had arrived. Gradually, the Desert Archaic people modified their migrations to have more time to plant and to tend their crops.

Contrary to popular belief, however, the hunter-gatherers appeared loath to become farmers. They enjoyed a bountiful natural harvest assembled with little effort, a fact testified to by repeated attempts by some prehistoric farmers to quit farming and return to hunting and gathering.

Even during modern times, hunter-gatherer people invest far fewer working hours than do urban dwellers.

Probably motivated solely by the need to find more dependable food supplies as population growth strained natural supplies, at least some of the Desert Archaic people made the slow transition from wanderers to settled farmers, and the foundation was established upon which later societies eventually were built.

Just as empires rose and fell in the Eastern Hemisphere for centuries prior to Columbus, so too did they rise and fall in the Americas.

And what made these civilizations especially astounding was the fact that they were built solely through human toil.

Unlike Europe, Asia, the Middle East, and Africa, the Americas had few animals suitable for domestication. There were no beasts of burden, except perhaps the dog in North America, and the llama and alpaca—capable of carrying only relatively small loads—in South America.

Moreover, because there were few animals suitable for agricultural use in the Americas and because only limited types of grains were available for cultivation compared with abundant arable grains found throughout Europe and Asia, the people of the Americas were at a nutritional disadvantage.

And with the north-to-south orientation of the two continents, temperate zones in North America were widely isolated from temperate zones in South America, limiting the diffusion of arable plants from one region to another. In the prehistoric Americas, for example, the potato never spread northward from its native Andes, while similar plants spread rapidly across thousands of miles of climatically similar Europe and Asia.

NAVAJO WOVEN JUG AND RUG,
COURTESY: CAMERON TRADING POST, ARIZONA

SQUARE HOUSE RUIN, MONUMENT VALLEY NAVAJO TRIBAL PARK, ARIZONA-UTAH

The Anasazi

Over 2,500 years ago, embers of what was to eventually become an impressive civilization began to smolder on the Colorado Plateau.

Originating out of the Desert Archaic tradition, the civilization finally burst into full flame, only to mysteriously falter a thousand years later.

Amazingly, though, vibrant remnants of this ancient culture still survive in the Southwest.

The people of this long-ago civilization are known today as the Anasazi, from the Navajo word, Anaasazi, which has been variously interpreted to mean "Ancient Tribe," "Ancient Enemy," or "Enemy Ancestors."

The Hopi people, some of the Anasazi's modern-day descendents, meanwhile, call them Hisatsinom, or "Long-Ago People."

What the Anasazi called themselves will probably remain one of the lost secrets of antiquity, or perhaps it is as obvious as the names some of the modern-day Pueblo people call themselves.

The Anasazi, or Hisatsinom, were a reddish-brown-haired or black-haired people of short, stocky stature, who lived primarily along the rugged expanses of the San Juan River drainage of the Colorado Plateau. However, theirs and related cultures also existed as far away as Nevada and northern Mexico.

The first evidence in the Four Corners area of the Anasazi as a distinct, identifiable group differing from other Desert Archaic people dates from about 500 B.C.

Sometime before 500 A.D., the first known permanent Anasazi village was built to the north of current-day Durango, Colorado, in a fertile, gentle valley cradled in the southern foothills of the San Juan Mountains and intersected by the deep,

35

rolling waters of the Animas River.

Like other Desert Archaic people, the Anasazi were hunter-gatherers, who planted crops to augment natural food supplies. Eventually, however, they settled down to devote more energy to cultivation.

Over a couple of centuries, many communities consisting of "pithouses"—rounded little dwellings resting partly above ground, partly below ground, and roofed with logs and a mud-and-clay mixture

ANASAZI RUIN, UTE MOUNTAIN TRIBAL PARK, COLORADO

that archeologists call "wattle-and-daub"— sprang up throughout the Four Corners area. Special pithouses, meanwhile, today known as kivas—Hopi for "sacred ceremonial chamber"— were built in the villages as religious structures.

This earliest stage of Anasazi development, called the Basketmaker era, was so named because, while the still-primitive people wove extremely intricate baskets and sandals, they lacked the ability to make pottery.

They cultivated fields of squash and corn, hunted wild animals, and harvested wild plants.

But by roughly 750 A.D., the Animas Valley and most other valleys in the region were abandoned, perhaps because of a period of damp summer weather that simultaneously made the river valleys cooler and more flood prone and the warmer mesa tops and desert more arable.

Between 500 A.D. and 700 A.D., the Anasazi began to cultivate beans, and by about 750 A.D., depending upon the individual community, because theirs was not a homogeneous society, the Anasazi culture began to flare into full intensity, the beginning of the Developmental Pueblo era.

It was then the Anasazi began to make pottery

and move their dwellings from the earth into the sun, as they abandoned their pithouses and instead constructed *pueblos*—Spanish for "town"—the beginning of a building tradition still in use across the Southwest.

The early pueblos, made of stone bonded with mud mortar, were simple rectangular-shaped, one-story structures, abutting one another, sharing one or two common walls, and usually facing south or southwest. The kivas of the Developmental Pueblo era, meanwhile, were moved deeper into the ground than their pithouse predecessors, were made larger, and were made with masonry and mortar walls, rather than wattle-and-daub.

Over the next few hundred years, the pueblos gradually became more elaborate until between 1100 A.D.—much earlier in one instance—and 1300 A.D., about the time Christians in distant Europe were launching the Crusades, they evolved into great multi-stories complexes of the Classic Pueblo era.

The Anasazi people of this time refined other skills, developing pottery with intricate designs in a multitude of colors; weaving fabrics out of cotton, perhaps grown by the Anasazi or perhaps purchased from people living in Arizona and central New Mexico; making elaborate jewelry of turquoise; extending systems of trade across hundreds of miles of the prehistoric Southwest and deep into Mexico; refining agriculture; and developing a complex religion that was integrated into every aspect of their lives.

The height of the Anasazi civilization had arrived.

The Chaco Phenomenon

Today, ruins of literally hundreds of long-ago Anasazi villages dot the Colorado Plateau. From the deep, secluded canyons of Utah and Arizona, to the lush, green foothills of Colorado's San Juan Mountains, to the sunburned desert of northwestern New Mexico, vestiges of sometimes awesome communities stand on wind-swept mesas and in the depths of the desert.

A thousand or more years ago, these communities began to flourish, not part of an extensive, closely knit, bureaucratic empire, but each a loosely bonded part of a cultural amalgam. The Anasazi people of widely disparate geographic regions probably didn't even speak the same language, although they shared other basic cultural traits. Individual communities, often isolated by great miles of Southwestern landscape, evolved and changed, motivated by the specific environmental, social, and cultural conditions of a particular region.

Some rocketed to greatness in a few short centuries, others plodded along unspectacularly, but dependably, to persevere, if not excel.

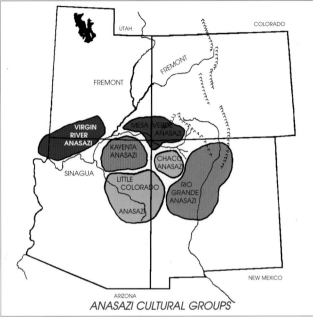

ANASAZI CULTURAL GROUPS

Archeologists recognize three major, distinct variations of the Anasazi culture, each named for the geographic locale where it evolved: the Chaco Canyon, Mesa Verde, and Kayenta cultural groups.

Three other cultural groups also occupied the area, the Virgin River Anasazi, in extreme southwest Utah and northwest Arizona north of the Grand Canyon; the Little Colorado Anasazi, to the southeast of the Grand Canyon along the Arizona-New Mexico border; and the Rio Grande Anasazi, along the upper Rio Grande River and its tributaries and along the drainage area of the eastern Rio Puerco between present-day Grants and Albuquerque, New Mexico. However, these three cultural groups were less archeologically distinct.

It was in fact at Chaco Canyon, New Mexico, today Chaco Culture National Historical Park and a United Nations World Heritage Site, that the Anasazi built the zenith of their civilization. But the Chaco culture, which rose like a mighty nova across the sky long before other Anasazi cultural centers, also darkened and died first, standing empty and abandoned while the Mesa Verde and Kayenta pueblos and cliff dwellings were still being built.

Chaco Canyon, almost exactly in the middle of the dry, sun-blistered San Juan Basin, is little more than a parched, rock-strewn ravine through which the Rio Chaco flows, usually nothing more than a feeble trickle of water moving west, then north, toward the San Juan River.

But by 900 A.D., about two centuries earlier than Anasazi elsewhere, Chaco was at the height of the Great Pueblo era.

Enormous pueblos were built along a roughly twenty-mile section of Chaco Canyon near Fajada Butte, a solitary monument protruding from the relative flatness of the San Juan Basin. Here, the Chaco Anasazi used elaborate water-control systems to carefully divert the region's marginal precipitation onto their crops.

Thirteen enormous pueblos, called "great houses," sometimes housing a thousand or more people each, stood at Chaco Canyon by 1000 A.D., reaching a combined peak population of about seven thousand people.

But the most awe-inspiring of all the pueblos was Pueblo Bonito, "Beautiful Village" in Spanish.

Construction on Pueblo Bonito began in 919 A.D. and continued for roughly 150 years. The pueblo eventually covered over three acres, was four stories high, contained eight hundred to nine hundred rooms, and housed upwards of one thousand people. Nearby Chetro Ketl—a Navajo term, which has never been precisely translated—was of roughly equivalent size.

The two structures comprised the most advanced pre-Colombian architecture in the United States.

And there were kivas, dozens of them, including "great kivas," religious structures up to sixty-three feet across and vastly larger than the average kiva or ten or twelve feet across.

PUEBLO BONITO, CHACO CULTURE NATIONAL HISTORICAL PARK

PUEBLO BONITO, CHACO CULTURE NATIONAL HISTORICAL PARK, NEW MEXICO

forms the real mystery of these prehistoric roads, originally photographed from the air by Charles Lindberg in the 1920s as part of a routine archeological survey—although recognized as highways in the early 1900s. The main arterial highways were roughly thirty-five feet wide, while smaller tributary highways were about half that, strangely wide for people without herd animals or wheeled vehicles.

The highways may provide the answer to one of the most baffling questions confronting archeologists: Why did the Chaco culture thrive in one of the driest, most inhospitable areas of the United States?

Archeologists theorize that the ancient highways may have been a lifeline.

Archeologists have discovered that at least forty communities scattered around the San Juan Basin were also constructed by the Chaco Anasazi. Among the largest of these "outliers" were two about thirty miles to the north, near present-day Aztec, New Mexico. Now known as the Aztec Ruins National Monument—also a United Nations World Heritage Site—and Salmon Ruin, both consisted of elaborate labyrinths of rooms used as residences, as well as many kivas, including great kivas.

One of the main characteristics of the Chaco outliers was that they were usually in areas of reliable water. Aztec Ruins National Monument, for example, rests on the banks of the Animas River, one of the largest rivers in the arid San Juan Basin. The people of this northern community cultivated crops on fertile lands near the Animas River.

During the early years of the Chaco communities, the Chacoans probably were able to grow adequate crops. As their population expanded, however, the Chaco Anasazi probably had to depend upon distant farms for supplies.

Near Dolores, Colorado, for example, rests another Chaco outlier, the Escalante Ruin. Located near the high San Juan Mountains and containing large amounts of bone fragments, it may have been a hunting outpost. Meanwhile, huge timber beams used as roof supports in the great houses and great kivas—over 200,000 roof beams at Chaco alone—salt, and other imported goods probably entered Chaco Canyon along its elaborate road system—imports purchased from neighboring Anasazi and people as distant as the

Casa Rinconada and Kin Nahasbas, standing independent of any pueblo, as well as great kivas within the actual pueblos, could probably easily accommodate one hundred or more worshippers. The kivas often were constructed partly or entirely above ground. In some pueblos, however, they were recessed into the pueblo superstructure, giving the illusion of being mostly below ground.

The stone work on Bonito-phase buildings—the most advanced Chacoan architecture—consisted of hundreds of thousands of carefully selected, finished, and chinked stones fitted to form a veneer over a center core of earth and stone rubble. Nearly a million such stones were meticulously fitted into the walls of Pueblo Bonito—detail work that was then hidden beneath plaster.

And the Chaco Anasazi apparently welcomed other Anasazi into the canyon to live and to trade, although perhaps only on a seasonal basis. Many ruins contemporary to Pueblo Bonito and Chetro Ketl, for example, were constructed by Anasazi from McElmo Canyon, Colorado, some one hundred miles northwest of Chaco and part of the Mesa Verde culture.

The Chacoans constructed the only known major network of prehistoric roads north of Mexico.

Meticulously built of stone or sometimes by removing soils to expose slickrock—or flat sandstone—formations, these baffling roads swept out across the San Juan Basin, straight and true regardless of terrain, their combined mileage probably exceeding five hundred miles.

The width, as much as the length, however,

Pacific coast, the Sea of Cortez, and Mexico.

The Chacoans probably paid for the commodities with turquoise, a semi-precious stone mined near Mount Taylor, along the southern rim of the San Juan Basin.

The Kayenta Cities

Nearly two hundred miles west-northwest of Chaco Canyon, the ruins of three incredibly beautiful Anasazi communities nestle in or near a seemingly out of place aspen-filled canyon, Tsegi Canyon, in the heart of the greater Painted Desert. This region, near today's Kayenta, Arizona, was the center of the Kayenta Anasazi culture, which blossomed later but survived longer than the Chaco culture.

The Kayenta people also were scattered across nearby Black Mesa, lived in the depths of the Grand Canyon, along the lower San Juan River drainage, and along the Escalanté River in extreme southern Utah.

But the three Kayenta towns at Tsegi Canyon—Betatakin (with 150 rooms, the largest cliff dwelling in Arizona), Keet Seel, and Inscription House—represent the height of the Kayenta culture and are now protected by Navajo National Monument.

Betatakin nestles under the shelter of an enormous sweep of Navajo Sandstone. Built about 1250 A.D., it is, partly because of its setting, one of the most beautiful cliff dwellings in the Southwest.

Although near the Colorado, Little Colorado, and San Juan rivers, the people of the Kayenta district lived on one of the driest parts of the Colorado Plateau. Unlike the Chaco Anasazi, they were far removed from the relatively moist, fertile regions bordering the arid San Juan Basin and were probably preoccupied with simple survival and had little time to achieve architectural and cultural excellence.

The various Anasazi architectural stages were not chronologically delineated in the Kayenta district, as in other cultural centers. It was not uncommon, for example, for some Kayenta Anasazi to live in pithouses next to others living in multi-story pueblos.

Probably the single most outstanding achievement of the Kayenta Anasazi was the development of vividly colored polychrome pottery. Black, white, and red geometric designs were laid down over yellow or orange backgrounds.

And while the Chaco Anasazi seemed preoccupied with building many kivas and extremely large kivas, the Kayenta Anasazi built comparatively few, and humble, religious structures. At Betatakin, for example, the Kayentans used only square, above-ground ceremonial structures, called *kihus*, rather than traditional kivas.

But though it may not have been as dynamic, the Kayenta culture survived long after Chaco Canyon was abandoned.

The Montelores Empire

Stretching from the current-day towns of Monticello and Blanding, Utah, on the west, to Cortez and Dolores, Colorado, on the east is one of the most fertile areas in the Southwest. This, the Montelores Plateau, sometimes also called the Great Sage Plain, is a four thousand square mile area tilted slightly south into the warming rays of the sun, a circumstance which prolongs the area's growing season in a land of short summers.

Not only is the soil, blown here by prevailing winds from across hundreds of miles of surrounding lands, extremely fertile, but the Montelores Plateau benefits from its proximity to the San Juan Mountains, receiving more precipitation than most of the rest of the Colorado Plateau.

Immediately to the southeast and towering some two thousand feet higher than the Montelores Plateau is the Mesa Verde.

On clear star-spackled nights a thousand years ago, the Anasazi living upon the high Mesa Verde plateau may have been able to see the signal fires of Chaco Canyon, some seventy miles to the southeast. Resting between the San Juan Mountains on the north and the greater Painted Desert to the south and the west, Mesa Verde commands a spectacular view of much of the San Juan Basin, Ship Rock, and lands beyond.

Early Spanish explorers, impressed by the

CLIFF PALACE, MESA VERDE NATIONAL PARK, COLORADO

mesa's lush greenness, called it, Mesa Verde, "Green Tableland." Gaining warmth off the desert and moisture off the nearby mountains, the roughly eighty square mile mesa is carpeted with piñon, juniper, Gambel oak, mountain mohagany, service berry, Fendler bush, and at higher elevations, ponderosa pine, Douglas fir, and aspen.

The Mesa Verde and the Montelores Plateau were home to the Mesa Verde, or Northern San Juan, Anasazi.

The highest population density, as well as the apex of the Mesa Verde culture, was on the Montelores Plateau, rather than on the now-famous Mesa Verde. Some pueblos, so far unexcavated, northwest of Cortez consisted of one thousand rooms or more, with perhaps as many as one hundred kivas in each pueblo.

HOVENWEEP NATIONAL MONUMENT, UTAH

The Yellow Jacket ruin had an estimated 1,820 rooms, 166 kivas, a great kiva, four plazas, twenty towers, and housed upwards of three thousand people, a much larger population than even Chaco Canyon's enormous Pueblo Bonito. Meanwhile, in 1990, another large ruin was discovered near Dove Creek, Colorado. The combined communities may have held a population of fifty thousand people, more than the area's present population.

But it is to the legendary Mesa Verde to which people from around the world trek, eager to see the amazing Anasazi cliff dwellings.

Ironically, these cliff dwellings, today protected within the boundaries of Mesa Verde National Park—another United Nations World Heritage Site—might have been built in response to a time of hardship that had befallen the Anasazi, hardship which was to eventually drive them from their homes in the Four Corners area. It was only during their final years in the area that the Anasazi built the cliff dwellings, as well as many of their most impressive—and baffling—free-standing pueblos.

Mesa Verde spreads like an enormous hand, with the palm toward the north, the fingers stretching south toward the desert. Between these fingers of higher land lie canyons, cut into the heights of the mesa by erosion. Each is lined with towering cliffs of sandstone and shale.

The first evidence of the Basketmaker Anasazi at Mesa Verde dates from about 550 A.D. By 1100 A.D., two hundred years later than at Chaco Canyon, Mesa Verde was in the Great Pueblo period.

The population at its height was about five thousand people.

Originally, the Mesa Verde Anasazi lived in pueblos scattered across the mesa top.

Although significantly smaller than the largest Chaco pueblos and of less refined construction, the Mesa Verde pueblos, such as Far View House, nonetheless were up to four stories high and were beautiful and awe-inspiring in their own right.

But abruptly about 1150 A.D., about the same time that the Chacoans were abandoning their desert cities, at least some of the Mesa Verdeans moved under the overhangs of the nearby cliff faces and began to build cliff dwellings.

The reason is unknown. Perhaps the cliff dwellings indicate nothing more sinister than a

SPRUCE TREE HOUSE RUIN, MESA VERDE

need to conserve wood during a time of shortages, since many of the cliff structures, sheltered by overhanging rock, needed no roofs.

Whatever the reason, the Mesa Verde cliff dwellings fitted hand-in-glove into the protective sandstone overhangs. Multi-story dwellings were

FOLLOWING PAGE:
AZTEC RUINS NATIONAL MONUMENT, NEW MEXICO

built toward the back of the pueblos; underground kivas, with plaza areas on top, toward the front.

Cliff Palace, the largest cliff dwelling, had 217 rooms, 23 kivas, and housed approximately 250 people.

The Exodus

But the Anasazi's attempt at adapting to adversity—whatever it might have been—was inadequate.

Chaco Canyon was abandoned by 1150 A.D. By 1300 A.D., Mesa Verde stood empty, although at least some Mesa Verde Anasazi lived among the abandoned cities of Chaco Canyon for a time.

Finally, even the diligent Kayenta Anasazi left Tsegi Canyon.

There have been many theories about what happened: drought, the spread of desertification triggered by agriculture-caused erosion, invading peoples, climate change, internal feuding, depletion of critical wood supplies, overpopulation or environmental degradation caused by overpopulation, or epidemics spread along trading routes or triggered by malnutrition.

Some archeologists and anthropologists believe that there is no simple answer, that a combination of some or all of these factors may have woven into an intricate web of conditions which eventually caused the Anasazi to move on. Perhaps the reasons for abandonment were not uniform, with the people of one village leaving for reasons that differed from those of neighboring villages.

One anthropologist and well-known author on the prehistoric Southwest, Dr. Linda Cordell, points out that, while the abandonment of cities in Europe rarely occurred, abandonment of population centers throughout the Americas was commonplace. In fact, only rarely were towns in the Southwest occupied for more than a few generations.

Among the Anasazi, it was the norm to abandon an area, probably when resources became strained by a growing population, by climate changes, or when too many years of cultivation decreased crop yields. The Anasazi occasionally reoccupied an area one or two centuries later, perhaps after the land healed or weather conditions had improved.

A paleoclimatologist involved in the 1980s in extensive excavations near Dolores, Colorado, where the U.S. Bureau of Reclamation's McPhee Dam flooded extensive Anasazi sites, advances another theory. Dr. Kenneth Peterson maintains that drought, combined with colder weather, was responsible.

From 600 A.D. to 750 A.D., the weather was warm and damp—nearly optimum—and the Anasazi thrived. About 750 A.D., a drought hit, albeit moderated by fairly heavy late-summer monsoons, and the Anasazi adapted by moving to higher, damper elevations, such as Mesa Verde.

By 1000 A.D. the climate again turned damp with continued moderate temperatures, and the Anasazi expanded cultivation to elevations down to 5,200 feet—to the depths of the San Juan Basin—an area nearly twice as extensive as that farmed today.

Soon, their culture reached its zenith.

But then, beginning about 1150 A.D., came a new drought, compounded by a lack of critical summer rain. The Chacoan cities—at low altitudes in the heart of the San Juan Basin—succumbed quickly, and then by 1200 A.D., the calamitous drought was compounded by temperature drops, preventing the Anasazi from cultivating crops in higher elevations, as they had in the earlier drought.

Meanwhile, the population had mushroomed. Even had high-altitude cultivation been possible, the lands of the Four Corners area might not have provided adequate food without the use of low-altitude lands.

The Anasazi were forced to leave. The evacuation was gradual, a slow withdrawal over many years, until by 1300 A.D., all the Anasazi were gone, the reason why they never returned as great a mystery as why they left.

PREVIOUS PAGE: WHITE HOUSE RUIN, CANYON DE CHELLY NATIONAL MONUMENT, ARIZONA

FAR VIEW RUIN, MESA VERDE NATIONAL PARK, COLORADO

43

LOMAKI RUIN, WUPATKI NATIONAL MONUMENT, ARIZONA

The Sinagua

During the winter of 1064-1065 A.D., a volcano erupted just northeast of today's city of Flagstaff, Arizona, spewing accumulations of ash and cinder across eight hundred square miles of the surrounding Wupatki Basin.

The Sinagua, a farming people, who, like the Anasazi originated out of the Desert Archaic culture, had lived in this area for at least five hundred years, but fled as their fields of corn, beans, and squash, and their pithouse homes, were destroyed by the onslaught.

Finally, about 1100 A.D., the Sinagua—Spanish for, "Without Water"—returned to their ancestral land and to what may have been fortune born of misfortune.

One theory about their return is that the thick accumulation of ash and cinder retained the region's marginal precipitation, both in the surface soil and in ground water, and slightly lengthened the growing season by warming the soil.

This warming, combined with a period of slightly damper weather, likely made Wupatki Basin nearly ideal for farming.

The Sinagua were rapidly joined by people of other nearby, closely related cultures, the Hohokam and Mogollon from the central mountain and desert regions of Arizona to the south; the Cohonina from the northwest, between the Colorado and Little Colorado rivers; and the Kayenta Anasazi.

Soon, hundreds of villages proliferated at what is now Wupatki National Monument, and later, at what is now nearby Walnut Canyon National Monument. Others flourished to the south, along the comparitively lush Verde River at what are now Tuzigoot--Apache for "Crooked Water"--and Montezuma Castle national monuments.

The cultures quickly blended into an amalgam, a colorful, thriving hybrid Sinaguan culture.

Multi-story pueblos, similar to those of the Anasazi, were constructed at Wupatki—a Hopi term variously translated to mean "Great Rain Cloud Ruin," "Tall House," or "Red Ruins in Black Cinder."

Wupatki Ruin, in particular, is a beautiful and amazing structure constructed in and around an outcropping of giant boulders. The ancient ruin represents an especially imaginative blend of setting and architecture, as the pueblo rests at the edge of an alluvial plain overlooking windswept desert mesas to the north.

A short way down the hill, a round ball court, a tradition originating in Central America and brought to northern Arizona by the Hohokam, was built, as was a round amphitheater, probably a kiva structure used for ceremonial or religious purposes.

Kivas of many shapes, sizes, and variations—round above-ground kivas, square below-ground kivas, and round below-ground kivas—were also built in the Wupatki Basin. Meanwhile, the Sinagua made elaborate turquoise ornaments. And unlike the Anasazi, who buried their dead in a fetal position, they partially cremated and then buried their dead with legs extended within narrow graves.

As the population grew, the overflow moved into nearby Walnut Canyon, where more than three hundred cliff dwelling-type rooms were built into limestone ledges along the canyon walls.

To the south, the Verde Valley Sinagua took advantage, at Montezuma Castle, of sheltering limestone cliffs into which they built cliff dwellings, and at Tuzigoot, of fertile river bottomlands to farm.

But by 1225 A.D., the Sinagua abandoned the area for reasons which are not entirely clear. One theory is that soil depletion, combined with a sustained drought, perhaps compounded by the wind blowing away much of the once-protective ash, may have caused the dispersal.

Like the towns of the Anasazi, the villages of the Sinagua amalgam ultimately rested empty and silent.

The Fremont

FREMONT ROCK ART, DINOSAUR NATIONAL MONUMENT, UTAH

They were here long, long ago, living in the canyons of the Colorado Plateau, drawing figures on sandstone walls, hunting animals in the desert and mountains.

Yet, beyond a few simple facts gleaned from the ruins and relics of their lifeway, little is known. The Fremont were the mystery people of the Colorado Plateau, their history a baffling conundrum that has perplexed archeologists as to their genesis and their eventual fate.

The Fremont—named in modern times after southern Utah's Fremont River—lived north and west of the Colorado River, spreading throughout northwest Colorado, Utah, and into Nevada at about the same time the Anasazi were spreading throughout the Four Corners area. They lived only as far south as the Waterpocket Fold and Fremont River in what is now Capitol Reef National Park in south-central Utah.

Did they evolve out of the Desert Archaic culture, as did the Anasazi? Were they a splinter group of the Anasazi? Or, since they seemed to share many of the same cultural traits—such as wearing moccasins, rather than sandals as did the Anasazi—were they Plains Indians who had found their way into Utah from eastern Colorado and Wyoming?

At present, the theory that they evolved from the Desert Archaic culture enjoys the broadest acceptance.

Before 500 A.D. the Fremont, like the Anasazi, lived in pithouses and cultivated crops, after having evolved from a strictly hunter-gatherer culture. However, they probably depended upon agriculture less and on hunting more than did the Anasazi.

Their buildings were never as grand as those of the Anasazi. They continued to live in pithouses, while their surface structures remained small and few in number, and they built no kivas. They did construct small granaries and storage pits, and they made lovely pottery, gray in its original color, but decorated with strips of clay molded into animal shapes or painted with geometric designs after firing.

They also made elaborate clay and wood figurines, probably for religious use, sometimes in pairs, male and female, or single figures representing a pregnant woman, or figures with human-like bodies and bird-like heads.

And they created hauntingly beautiful rock art on desert cliff faces, at Dinosaur National Monument and Canyonlands, Capitol Reef, and Arches national parks and elsewhere. The rock art depicted wildlife and human figures, some drawn to appear to be carrying likenesses of human heads. (Some rock art in these regions, such as the spectacular Great Gallery in Canyonlands National Park, predates even the Fremont people by several thousand years.)

But the final mystery of the Fremont is what became of them after they, like the Anasazi, left the isolated canyons of Utah by about 1300 A.D.

They may have cast off the burden of building stone dwelling places and farming and returned to a strictly hunter-gatherer culture, wandering the desert and mountains of Utah and Colorado, perhaps the ancestors of today's Utes or Southern Paiutes.

Perhaps they returned to the Great Plains to hunt buffalo and live as nomads. Or, perhaps they moved south, as did the Anasazi.

What became of them is as enigmatic as the strange rock art figures that they left behind.

PICTURES ON ROCKS

GREAT GALLERY PICTOGRAPHS, CANYONLANDS NATIONAL PARK, UTAH

It is one of the surprising gifts of the Southwest to look up in some familiar place and for the first time see an ancient figure—perhaps normally hidden in shadows or by the branch of a tree—carved into the surface of a rock.

Many have a vibrant and continuing significants to present-day Indians, especially the Pueblos, who revere them for religious reasons and as a link to the past.

The meaning of literally thousands of these ancient images is not fully understood and likely never will be. Perhaps they were used to communicate—to warn of danger or to tell of wild game or water nearby. Perhaps they were religious icons, or maybe they were created simply for the joy of creating. Likely, they were each of these things, depending upon location and circumstance.

There are two types of rock art, "petroglyphs," figures carved onto a rock surface or into the black manganese oxide or brown iron oxide, known as desert varnish, coating rock surfaces. And there are "pictographs," painted images made of charcoal or of mineral- or plant-based paints.

Such figures were created literally over the span of thousands of years.

The oldest rock art dates from the Paleo Indians, who lived on the Colorado Plateau at least ten thousand years ago, and who left petroglyphs depicting ice age mammoths—which they probably hunted to extinction—along the Colorado River near Canyonlands National Park and near Moab, Utah.

And there is the rock art left by the Desert Archaic people, perhaps up to eight thousand years ago, long before the Anasazi and Fremont people. Some of the most haunting and dramatic of this vintage—or any vintage—are those of a small little-known fringe culture, the Barrier Canyon people, who likely created the towering, mummy-like figures eight feet or more tall, of the Great Gallery, in the Horseshoe Canyon unit of Canyonlands National Park and in a few other remote canyons in southeast Utah.

The Anasazi, meanwhile, left a proliferation of figures: hummingbirds, spirals, animals, comets, suns, faces, handprints, and perhaps most famous, kokopelli.

This nearly ubiquitous humpbacked flute player—usually sexually well-endowed and with a nearly perpetual erection—spans Anasazi history from the early Basketmakers through to the present-day Hopis, who represent him ceremonially as a kachina.

Perhaps a fertility figure, kokopelli is often alone, but elsewhere, such as near Bandelier National Monument, dozens dance across the smoke-stained ceiling of a cave kiva.

The Anasazi and other people of the Colorado Plateau—the Utes, Navajos, Paiute, Pai, and later, the Spaniards and American settlers—created sometimes dramatic clusterings of rock art, especially at Newspaper Rock, near the entrance to the Needles District of Canyonlands, and at El Morro and Petroglyph national monuments in New Mexico.

But sadly, present-day people are contributing to rock art in other, less kindly ways. A spectacular panel containing Barrier Canyon and other pictographs—the Moab Panel at the south edge of Arches National Park—was nearly destroyed by vandals in 1980.

They used abrasives to nearly obliterate figures painted on a sandstone surface, including several hauntingly beautiful Barrier Canyon figures similar to those at the Great Gallery, only with strange, arching horns on their heads. The vandals then carved obscenities into the panel surface.

Dr. Constance Silver, an art restoration-expert, partially reconstructed the Moab Panel. During the work, she found even older art beneath the surface drawings. But despite her work, the panel, under a protective overhang where it otherwise would have likely endured for centuries, will never again boast bright colors and sharply defined figures.

46

RECONSTRUCTED GREAT KIVA, AZTEC RUINS NATIONAL MONUMENT, NEW MEXICO

The Pueblos

When the Anasazi left the Four Corners area, it was not the end of them nor their way of life, merely a transition, a time when they moved on into a new era.

The Anasazi were the ancestors of those known today as the Pueblo people—the Hopis of northeastern Arizona, the Zuni, Acoma, and Laguna Pueblo people to the west of Albuquerque, New Mexico, and the Rio Grande Pueblo people, along the Rio Grande Valley of north-central New Mexico.

The Pueblo villages that dot the plateaus and river valleys of northern New Mexico and northern Arizona are manifestations of the living continuum of the Anasazi tradition. Although the people of the various villages often speak different languages, as their Anasazi ancestors probably did, they share the same basic cultural traits and the same general Anasazi ancestry.

PREVIOUS PAGE: TAOS PUEBLO, NEW MEXICO

From the Mesa Verde, Chaco Canyon, and Kayenta regions, the Anasazi dispersed southeast, south, and southwest to places, in most cases, already inhabited by others of their numbers.

The present-day Hopi village of Oraibi, for example, existed in 1100 A.D., a time when the Anasazi still lived at Kayenta, Mesa Verde, and Chaco Canyon. Oraibi may have existed in some form a thousand years before that, while Acoma—called New Mexico's "Sky City"—on a promontory towering more than three hundred feet higher than the surrounding desert—has been occupied for at least eight hundred years, perhaps much longer. Acoma means, "place that always was."

But the places to which specific cultural groups moved remains a mystery.

Archeologists have examined clues and anthropologists have studied migration legends of modern-day Pueblo people, largely in vain, to find proof of which Anasazi cultural group went where during the dispersal.

What archeologists do know is that, as the Anasazi left the Four Corners, there were significant increases in the populations of many already established pueblo communities.

Probably, since the Anasazi people dispersed a few at a time—perhaps a few individuals or even an entire clan group at once—rather than by community-wide evacuations, they scattered widely, going to live in or near established communities where they already had friends or family.

The Hopi people believe that they are variously the descendents of the Kayenta and Sinagua Anasazi, perhaps confirmed in part by present-day, square-shaped Hopi kivas, or kihus, although some Hopi verbal tradition also states that they are descended from Colorado's Mesa Verde Anasazi.

It may not be coincidental that the Hopi villages, except for Hano—made up of Tewa-speaking people from northern New Mexico—speak a Uto-Aztecan language, as do the Utes, who also lived in the area of Mesa Verde in antiquity. The Hopi call their Greasewood Clan "Utes"—tradition has it because they lived near and associated with the Utes.

Some of the Chacoans, meanwhile, may have moved to present-day Acoma, roughly seventy miles south of Chaco Canyon, or to Zuni, twenty or thirty miles due south of Gallup. The largest surviving pueblo in the Southwest, Zuni boasts elaborate stonework similar to that at Chaco.

Archeologists call the period of migration, between 1300 A.D. and 1600 A.D., the Regressive, or Renaissance, Pueblo era.

The Anasazi culture did not eclipse or slip into obscurity. In fact, of all of the Anasazi cultural divisions, only the Chaco culture declined, and at the time of Coronado's expedition of 1540, the Spaniards found roughly one hundred inhabited Pueblo villages, mostly along the Rio Grande. They also found evidence of literally hundreds of other previously inhabited communities.

In the Galisteo Basin near Santa Fe, a number of enormous post-exodus and pre-Colombian pueblos stood in the brightness of the New Mexico sun. Pueblo Colorado had 881 rooms on the ground floor alone, Pueblo Shé featured 1,543 ground-floor rooms—much bigger than Pueblo Bonito at Chaco Canyon. Pueblo Blanco had 1,450 first-floor rooms, and San Lazaro 1,900.

About forty miles to the north in 1450 A.D., stood Poseoungie, a modern-day Tewa Pueblo Indian word meaning "stinking water," probably after the foul smell, at the time, of the nearby Ojo Caliente hot springs. This enormous pueblo, sprawled in two huge sections on a rise overlooking the Rio Ojo Caliente, probably had two thousand rooms, but was nonetheless smaller than the nearby El Rito complex, believed by some to have been the largest pueblo in the Southwest at the time—as one local cowboy recently described them, not "lightweight pueblos. These were big cities."

UNIDENTIFIED PUEBLO WOMAN, TAOS PUEBLO, NEW MEXICO
COURTESY: COLORADO HISTORICAL SOCIETY

The people of these pueblos—inhabited until about 1540, fifty years before the Spaniards arrived—did dryland farming, raising crops on flat ground near arroyos by mulching the ground with thousands of small pebbles to retain the moisture. They also built check dams to use rainwater to create moist basins in which to raise crops.

In contrast, today there are only thirty occupied Pueblo villages: the Hopi villages of Walpi, Sitchumovi, Shungopovi, Shipaulovi, Mishongnovi, Oraibi, Moencopi, Hotevilla, Bacabi, Kykotsmovi, and Hano, with a population of just over seven thousand people.

And there are the New Mexico villages of Zuni, Acoma, and Laguna, west of Albuquerque, and the nearby Rio Grande-area villages of Zia, Santa Domingo, Santa Ana, San Felipe, Cochiti, Sandia, and Isleta. Further north, there is the Jemez pueblo, at the base of the Jemez Mountains, while villages further north along the Rio Grande, are San Juan, Santa Clara, San Ildefonso, Tesuque, Nambé, Pojoaque, Picuris, and Taos. These villages have a combined population of about 25,000 people.

The Conquest

When the Spanish Conquistadores moved north from Mexico, they undoubtedly represented a frightening sight to the Indians of the Southwest.

The Spaniards wore strange metal armor, carried guns—which they took delight in discharging—and rode horses, animals long extinct in the Americas and never before seen by the Indians.

The first Pueblo village seen by Europeans was in 1539, when Fray Marcos de Niza, an Italian in service of Spain, guided by a Moor by a the name of Estaban, led an expedition in search of the legendary Seven Cities of Cíbola, mythical cities of gold that had been part of Spanish lore since the ninth century.

Estaban was killed by the people of Zuni, and de Niza, waiting in view of the pueblo and hearing of the death, fled back to Mexico, convinced that he had seen one of the legendary cities of gold.

De Niza was followed the next year by the Coronado expedition, during which Coronado and his men massacred the entire pueblo village of Tiguex on the Rio Grande.

The colonizing mission of Juan de Oñate, meanwhile, arrived in 1598, and in 1610 Santa Fe was founded, beginning the so-called Historic Pueblo era, a time of profound suffering for the Pueblo people.

Many were sold into slavery, while the Spanish confiscated crops, raped, pillaged, pastured their hor-ses in Pueblo fields, and exacted exorbitant duties, usually in the form of food, since the Spaniards were often unable to fend adequately for themselves in the rugged land. At times the duties became so unreasonable that the Pueblos themselves starved.

The Spaniards also attempted to destroy the Pueblo religion, a complicated set of ceremonies, traditions, and beliefs guiding all aspects of Pueblo government, social life, crop planting, and harvesting. In many pueblos, the Spaniards filled the sacred kivas with dirt.

Those Pueblo people who resisted the invasion were flogged, hanged, or sometimes burned alive.

At Acoma, which unsuccessfully withstood a prolonged siege in defiance of the Spaniards, hundreds died. After their conquest, each surviving warrior had a foot hacked off by the Spaniards to thwart further resistance. Two Hopi warriors captured at Acoma each had a hand cut off and were sent home as an example of

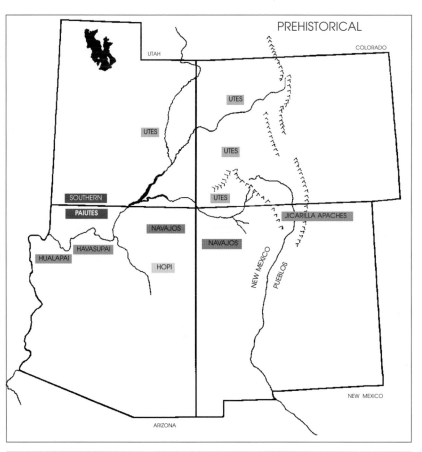

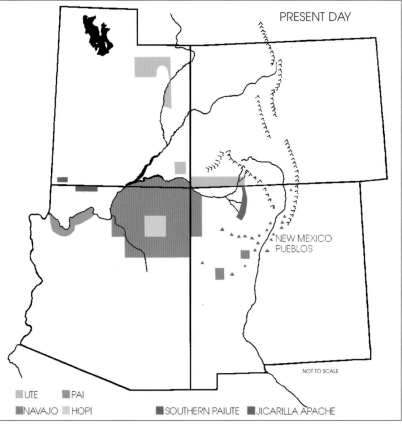

50

PECOS MISSION, PECOS NATIONAL HISTORICAL PARK, NEW MEXICO

Some four hundred Spanish settlers and eighteen priests were killed by the enraged Pueblos, the rest—after the Pueblos laid siege to the Spanish capitol of Santa Fe—were allowed to flee south along the Rio Grande. But the Pueblos paid dearly to gain their freedom, losing 350 people, 47 of them captured and executed by the Spaniards before the Spaniards fled south to El Paso.

After the revolt, Pueblos held the Spaniards at bay for twelve years, until 1692, when Diego de Vargas Ponce de León reconquered the New Mexico Pueblos.

The Arizona pueblos were different. The Hopis firmly resisted reoccupation and were never reconquered.

The price of the Pueblos' brief taste of freedom was high. At the Tano Pueblo in the Galisteo Basin south of Santa Fe, eighty some people were executed for resisting the Spaniards' return, while six hundred others from various villages were sold into slavery in the West Indies, never to see their homes, families, or beloved Southwest again.

For some Pueblo people, Spanish domination became intolerable. Many fled their Rio Grande-area homes.

what resistance would bring.

Authorities in Mexico City ultimately banished Oñate back to Spain, in part to punish him for the atrocities he committed in New Mexico.

The Spaniards also inadvertently introduced measles, smallpox, and other European diseases, to which the Pueblos and other Indians had no immunity. The results were catastrophic. Many Indian populations, to this day, have not recovered from the resulting deaths.

In Mexico, for example, 3.5 million people died of smallpox within a year of the arrival of Hernan Cortés—who conquered the Aztecs of Mexico in 1521. The Pueblo people, meanwhile, confined in towns and therefore particularly vulnerable to disease, declined so radically in population that by 1700 only eighteen of the original one hundred pueblos seen in New Mexico in 1540 remained. In the late nineteenth century, a handful of survivors in one Hopi pueblo—ill themselves—shoved the dead off cliffs lining their mesa-top home, after American miners and settlers exposed the village to smallpox.

Finally, in 1680, after a previous unsuccessful uprising in 1642, the Pueblos, with the help of the Apaches, revolted and drove the Spaniards out. Led by Popé of the San Juan Pueblo, the revolt spread to all of the Pueblo villages, even to Arizona's Hopi mesas, the only time in recorded history that the many autonomous villages acted in unison.

ACOMA PUEBLO, NEW MEXICO

The Ancient Ways

In 1696, Jemez Pueblo unsuccessfully revolted and was ultimately abandoned for a time, as its people fled to live among the Navajos. In fact, to this day, Navajos of the Coyote Pass clan trace much of their ancestry to Jemez.

Later, in 1838, the last twenty members of the once-impressive Pecos Pueblo east of Santa Fe—now Pecos National Historical Park—migrated west to Jemez Pueblo, leaving the already deteri-

CORN DANCER, SAN JUAN PUEBLO, NEW MEXICO,

orating pueblo and its huge Spanish church to fall to ruin.

Other residents of Rio Grande-area pueblos, meanwhile, were invited to establish a village among the Hopis—today's village of Hano.

And during the four hundred years since the Spanish reconquest, the Pueblos' beloved Southwest has continued to remain occupied, first by Spain until 1820, then Mexico until 1835, and finally, by the United States.

The best way to appreciate the Pueblo tradition is to view the beauty of age-old pueblos and to observe a way of life through which the Anasazi and their descendents have persevered.

However, because of intrusions on the Pueblos'

privacy, visitors are unwelcome in some villages and in some others may enter only under special conditions. Photography is always banned without permission.

In the rapidly growing Southwest—according to the United Nations, the United States in 1999 was the sixth fastest growing nation in the world—the Pueblos' culture is experiencing unparalleled pressures, from encroaching development and the onslaught of the surrounding predominant industrial American culture. And as anywhere else in the United States, drug use, alcoholism, increased crime, teen pregnancy, and pop culture intrude daily.

Some villagers consider themselves to be traditionalists and try to adhere strictly to the old ways and to hold the outside world at bay. Others, the so-called progressives, see embracing parts of surrounding cultures, while trying to preserve select parts of their own ways.

But for now in the pueblos—often large, sprawling complexes the color of the desert earth—ladders still protrude from kivas and children run through the complicated maze of streets as generations of children before them must have.

At the Rio Grande pueblos and in the shadow of Mount Taylor to the west of Albuquerque, churches built by the conquering Spaniards protrude from the depths of the villages. However, Spanish missions built among the Hopi villages were demolished by the Hopis in the wake of the Pueblo Revolt and were never permitted to be rebuilt.

But another vestige of the Spanish years and, later, the Mexican and American influence, remains with tribal government at the New Mexico pueblos.

In 1620, under a decree from the King of Spain, secular offices—including a governor and two lieutenant governors—were established to administer each pueblo. A metal-topped cane was given to each pueblo as a symbol of authority for those offices.

When Mexican independence was won from Spain in 1821, a new cane was given to each New Mexico pueblo, followed in 1863, by yet another cane, presented to the tribes—and inscribed with his name—by Abraham Lincoln to thank them for their neutrality in the Civil War.

Most of the canes are still retained in the pueblos, sometimes with others subsequently added to the collection, as symbols of secular pueblo government.

And in keeping with ancient tradition, there are the fields which still provide much of the food for the pueblos.

In the Rio Grande Valley, fields are cultivated

ZUNI DANCERS, GALLUP INTERTRIBAL INDIAN CEREMONIAL, GALLUP, NEW MEXICO

along the fertile bottomlands, where it is easy to divert water for irrigation. However, on the sun-baked Hopi mesas of northern Arizona, most of the fields of corn, beans, squash, peach trees, and cotton are unirrigated, with the exception of those at Moenkopi, the western-most village. The only pueblo located off of the three Hopi mesas, it rests along the intermittent waters of Moenkopi Wash.

On average, only about twelve inches of moisture annually falls on the semi-arid Hopi mesas, the driest part of the Colorado Plateau. Yet, crops survive both because of the prudent use of water and, the Hopis say, because of their meticulous adherence to religious tradition.

With the wisdom of ages spent on the Colorado Plateau, the Hopis—often using traditional digging sticks, as did their ancestors before them—plant their crops deeply, sometimes a foot or more into the sandy soil, sheltering seeds and roots from the drying winds of the Painted Desert.

Other crops are planted on sometimes elaborately terraced and walled areas along the edges of the mesas. Rainwater running off the mesa, pueblo rooftops, and streets finds its way onto the terraces below, while walls protect crops from the relentless wind. Stunted little peach trees and corn, meanwhile, grow in the alluvial plains at the base of the mesas, where both surface and underground runoff from the mesas flows.

Other age-old customs also survive.

Pueblo women still own all household property and the seeds for planting. Girl babies are often preferred over boys by expectant parents, who look at them as essential to the perpetuation of the clan, several of which comprise each Arizona or New Mexico pueblo.

Clan membership is determined matrilineally, or through the female line, and a couple settles matrilocally, or with the wife's family.

Since a married couple adhering to the traditional ways often settles in the house owned by a woman's mother and her mother's mother before her, it is not uncommon for a woman to live her entire life in one house. In some cases, as at Zuni, although the men do all of the farm work, the women own the resulting crops.

However, in the highly communal villages of the Pueblo people, ownership does not imply the same connotations as it does in other economies.

As in the time of the Anasazi, the men do the weaving, often in the kivas, which are owned by the men and form the center of religious ceremony, social activities, and craft work.

In some of the pueblos, the village is divided in half down the middle from east to west, with the north half of the village consisting of the winter people and the south half, the summer people; or in some cases, the turquoise people and the squash people. These divisions, at least in New Mexico, are usually led by a *cacique*, a leader chosen to serve for life. The most dramatic example of this village division—as can be readily seen in the physical structure of the pueblo is at Taos, where the pueblo is built on either side of a large plaza intersected by a small stream.

The beautiful Pueblo villages, meanwhile, reflect a centuries-old building tradition. In many villages, the women do much of the stone work, leading archeologists to believe that the detailed masonry at Chaco Canyon may have been done by the Anasazi women.

The Age-Old Faith

Pueblo life is centered around religious beliefs with roots going back into the antiquity of the Colorado Plateau.

In the New Mexico pueblos, faith also is tied to Roman Catholicism, accepted by the people alongside their traditional beliefs or sometimes integrated with these traditional beliefs.

Traditional Pueblo religion dominates virtually every aspect of life. In fact, there is often no practical distinction between the secular and the religious.

Village civic leadership and religious leadership are either one and the same, or secular leaders are strongly influenced by village religious leaders.

As in the time of the Anasazi, solar astronomy plays an important role in predicting the solstices, the equinoxes, and other seasonal sacred occasions. A day rarely passes without an important religious observance, part of a complicated, interrelated web of ritual and ceremony closely integrated to the passing of the seasons. To chart these ceremonies, the sun's progress—from north to south in summer, south to north in winter—along the eastern horizon at dawn is carefully watched.

It is a religion so bewilderingly intricate that anthropologists who have studied it still have only a cursory understanding of it—in part because the Pueblos, to protect the integrity and strength of their beliefs, keep many articles of faith secret.

The Pueblos—whose religion profoundly influenced the beliefs of other indigenous people of the Colorado Plateau—believe that rather than migrating from Asia via the Bering Strait, they climbed to the surface of this world from a world below. They honor six sacred directions, north, east, south, and west, plus the upper world of the living, and the lower world of the dead.

The sun rises from his house in the east, journeys across the sky, lighting this world, then sets in his house in the west, and from there travels back to the east, lighting the underworld while he moves.

The point of original emergence, as exemplified by the *sipapu*, a symbolic hole at the bottom of a kiva, leads to the underworld from which the Pueblo people emerged during remote antiquity and to which the dead return within a few days of death. The two worlds are not considered to be separate but part of a continuum, with reciprocity and communication between the two through the spirits of the dead, who can move easily from one to the other.

The Pueblos see the universe as animate, with virtually everything in it having a spiritual essence. The natural, the supernatural, the living, the dead, humans, animals, plants, the Earth, sun, moon, clouds, rocks, trees, water, even food, have a spiritual essence.

ORGE KACHINA DOLL
COURTESY: LEMA TRADING POST, MOAB, UTAH
KACHINA MADE BY HOIPI ARTIST HARRY BERT

All things are interrelated and mutually dependent. Most elements operate automatically, guided by the dynamics of the universe; however, humankind, by living properly, can positively influence events and can communicate with the

KIVA, PECOS NATIONAL HISTORICAL PARK, NEW MEXICO

forces of nature and with the sun through prayer sticks, or *pahos*, small sticks with sacred eagle feathers attached, each carrying forth a message on the wind.

The Pueblos believe that elaborate rituals help to keep the world in harmony. Ceremonies are performed to encourage the supernatural beings to positively influence nature. The greatest divinity of all is symbolized by the sun and the lesser divinities, the kachinas, are thought to be the spirits of the dead.

Kachinas—popularly pronounced ka-chee'-nahs, but some say more properly pronounced kat'she-nahs, although pronunciation also varies between the pueblos—were not always part of the Pueblo religion. Kachina cults probably began between 1350 and 1540, during the Renaissance Pueblo era.

The Pueblos believe that kachinas—at Zuni, *shalako*—are linked to the coming of rain, the growing of crops, and the general well-being of the pueblo. Kachinas are kind, caring, compassionate beings, who reside in sacred lakes, streams, springs, or on mountain tops.

When they come to dance—represented by Pueblo men dressed in kachina costumes—it is believed they cause the rains to fall, vitally important in this harsh, dry land. In fact, many religious ceremonies are linked to the bringing of rain.

The Pueblos believe the kachinas themselves used to come to dance among the Pueblos. But some of the people took the kachinas for granted or fought with them, causing the kachinas to leave, but not before they taught some of the young, faithful men how to dance the kachina ceremonies. It is believed that if a dancer is good and pure, the kachina he impersonates will actually return to possess him as he performs the kachina dance.

Kachina masks, worn by the kachina dancers, have been handed down along family lines for generations—the Pueblos say, since time began, although some of the masks are sometimes technically community owned.

And, as in the lives of their Anasazi ancestors before them, the kiva is still the center of religious activity. In fact, the building and maintenance of a kiva are believed to be sacred acts, analogous to prayer.

The men of the village belong to particular kiva societies, with membership often determined by

DOOR, TAOS PUEBLO, NEW MEXICO

heredity.

The kiva contains a firepit with a ventilation shaft, an entrance—usually a ladder through the ceiling—and a sipapu in the floor. The kiva symbolizes the world below from which the Pueblos emerged. To leave the kiva via the ladder is a symbolic reenactment of that emergence.

The religious societies within a pueblo each have specific responsibilities aimed at maintaining balance and order in the universe. The status of these all-male societies is based upon the importance of the ceremonies they perform.

In the Hopi villages, for example, the Soyal Society performs one of the most important religious observances, the winter solstice ceremony, during which the sun, deep on the southern horizon, is guided into the beginning of his return journey to the north. Therefore, the Soyal holds perhaps the single greatest ceremonial responsibility.

In the Rio Grande pueblos, the beginning of the new year—and the return of the sun—is encouraged as all fires are extinguished during the winter solstice and then relit, analogous to the sun dimming in winter and then growing brighter with the approach of spring.

Membership in religious societies is looked upon as a responsibility toward the well-being of the pueblo. Crop plantings, for example, are precisely determined by religious protocol to give plants the optimum amount of time to ripen before the killing frosts of autumn.

Each year, beginning with the winter solstice, the kachinas intermittently appear in the Hopi villages. Each appearance throughout the following months is of tremendous spiritual importance, meant to assure the kachinas that the Hopi people are trying to live a pure and good life and are worthy of the kachinas' efforts on their behalf. Finally, in late July, the kachinas appear in the villages for the last time before returning to the heights of the San Francisco Peaks, some eighty miles to the southwest near Flagstaff, Arizona. There the kachinas will prepare to bring rain to the Hopis' crops during the rainy season of late July, August, and early September.

It is during these final visits that an important

and solemn ceremony is conducted, during which Hopi brides are presented to the kachinas. For the ceremony, each bride wears a white cotton robe woven by her husband's uncles.

Each woman also wears the same robe when she ceremonially presents her first-born child to the sun, at dawn twenty days after the child's birth. Finally, when the woman dies, she is buried in another white robe, which she held in her arms on the day she was married.

Resolutely, beautifully, a centuries-old way of life endures.

THE CONQUEROR'S FOOT

New Mexico is still trying to come to terms with some of the events of the Spanish *entrada*.

On a dark, cold January night in 1998, a year during which New Mexico officials planned observances to mark the *cuartocentenario*, the four-hundredth anniversary of the Spaniards' arrival, someone—it is rumored a group of Acoma Indians—sneaked into the grounds of the pink-stuccoed Oñate Visitors Center a few miles north of Española.

There, they sawed the right foot off a bronze statue of Don Juan de Oñate, astride a horse and looking grandly across the Española Valley.

The act—which earned front-page coverage in New Mexico newspapers—unleased anger and controversy.

Some Hispanic leaders were incensed at what they called a senseless act of vandalism at the very beginning of their year-long celebration of the Spaniards' arrival. But other New Mexicans felt, even four hundred years after the fact, that Oñate had it coming, and then some.

Although the statue has since been repaired, some argued at the time that tax dollars should not be spent replacing the damaged foot until an election or full public hearing was held to see how New Mexicans felt about the expenditure.

Wrote one Acoma resident to *The Santa Fe New Mexican*, "While Oñate may be a hero to some, to many of my people he embodied the worst that a person is capable of. People will say he was a product of that time. I do not believe that should be an excuse. When Oñate ordered that the right foot of the men at Acoma be cut off, it wasn't for protection of the Spanish, but rather for revenge."

Others argued the foot should be left off the statue as a symbolic reminder of Oñate and his time.

However, one descendent of two soldiers of Oñate's army argued that the vandalism was "but another manifestation of the cultural and historical rape of indigenous Hispanic New Mexico. This hatred of everything Spanish and (of) Spanish Americans must stop."

But the battle of the statues was just beginning.

About the same time, Indian activists asked that a statue or their "counter *conquestador*," Popé—the San Juan Pueblo warrior who led the bloody Pueblo revolt of 1680—be placed in the nation's capitol.

Nonsense, some Hispanics replied. The man responsible for the deaths of so many Spanish citizens during the 1680 revolt and siege of Santa Fe should not be honored, they said.

But in the midst of this controversy, middle ground could be found, as shown by the fact that so many Anglos, Hispanics, and Pueblo Indians today live in relative harmony in Northern New Mexico.

As one woman also wrote *The New Mexican*, "Several years ago, my husband and I were hiking on Cerro Pedernal (a mountain near Abiquiu, New Mexico). On the summit, we met two Hispanic men and their dog. They explained that they liked to make a pilgrimage now and then to this sacred Indian shrine to give thanks to the Indians who had saved their Spanish ancestors. 'If the Indians hadn't shown us how to survive in this hard land...we wouldn't be alive today,'" they told the couple.

OÑATE STATUE, ESPAÑOLA, NEW MEXICO
PHOTOGRAPH: KATHLEENE PARKER

GRAND CANYON NATIONAL PARK, ARIZONA   INSET: NAVAJO CHILD

The Navajos

A Navajo woman weaving a blanket or a Navajo man riding a horse across a desert sand dune are images virtually symbolic of the American Southwest.

Yet, compared with the Pueblo people who have lived on the Colorado Plateau for thousands of years, the Navajo are relative newcomers.

The earliest conclusively proven Navajo settlement, found in northwest New Mexico's Gobernador Canyon, dates from about 1541 A.D., although the remains of what may have been Navajo homes, dating from before 1000 A.D., have also been found in western Colorado. Many archeologists believe the Navajos were not in the Southwest before 1300 A.D.

All that is known with certainty is that some time during antiquity, for reasons which will probably never be known, people from western Canada began to find their way southward in small bands, perhaps along the eastern foothills of the Rocky Mountains, perhaps through western Colorado or eastern Utah, perhaps through the Great Basin region of Nevada and western Utah, or more probably, straggling in along several different routes over a period of generations, a fact partially confirmed by Navajo myths and verbal tradition.

These early Athabascan-speaking people were the ancestors of today's Navajo and Apache people, who to this day can understand at least some of the language of the Sekani people of Canada.

REMNANTS OF STICK HOGAN, MONUMENT VALLEY NAVAJO TRIBAL PARK

from the Pueblos, probably when the Navajos sheltered Pueblo refugees in the wake of the Pueblo Revolt.

The Navajos first officially began to be recognized as a distinctive people in 1626 when Fray Zarata-Salmeron referred to them as being separate from other Apaches, and in 1630 when Fray Alonso de Benavides, while writing to Spain, spoke of the distinction between them and other Apaches.

Using the Spanish spelling for the Tewa term he had heard, or thought he had heard, Benavides wrote of the Apachu de Navajo, thus the term "Navajo."

The Navajos nonetheless think of themselves not as Navajos, but as the Diné, the "People," or the "Earth Surface People," a name based on their belief that long ago, rising through a hole somewhere deep in the San Juan Mountains, their gods found a way to the surface of this world from a world below, then created the Diné.

Early Navajos on the Colorado Plateau built forked-stick hogans, round dwellings consisting of wooden poles leaned together at the peak and then plastered over with grass, sticks, and mud—structures similar to the pole dwellings, covered with branches and leaves, of the Canadian Athabascans.

From lush Canadian coastal areas, the migrating Athabascans, or at least their descendents, slowly found their way onto the arid expanses of the Colorado Plateau, where at first they were exclusively hunter-gathers. But that soon changed.

Strangers of the Fields

The Tewa-speaking Pueblo people—those of the northern New Mexico villages of Santa Clara, San Ildefonso, Pojoaque, Nambé and Tesuque and the Hopi village of Hano—originally named the newcomers, Apachu, meaning "Strangers" or "Enemies." But one group of Apaches they referred to differently. They called them the Apachu de Nabahu, "Strangers of the Cultivated Fields."

At least some of the Apaches, probably those living in or near the Rio Grande Valley—"The Land of the Corn Growers"—learned to farm, likely from the Pueblo people. In fact, the adaptable Navajos learned to imitate the Pueblos' urban way of life by sometimes grouping their hogans together in communities of fifty or more, with fields nearby. Sometimes hogan communities and pueblos stood side by side.

The Navajos likely also learned to weave

NAVAJO WARRIOR AND MEDICINE MAN, BI-JOSHII, CIRCA: 1920

HISTORICAL WILLIAM M. PENNINGTON PHOTOGRAPH
COURTESY: FORT LEWIS COLLEGE, CENTER FOR SOUTHWEST STUDIES, DURANGO, COLORADO

But they were not to remain sedentary farmers.

In 1598, Don Juan de Oñate headed his colonizing mission into the northern Rio Grande Valley from Mexico. In addition to 130 troops, the contingent consisted of priests, families, and retainers to bring the number of settlers to four hundred.

But perhaps just as important, a great cloud of dust rose skyward as the assembly traveled along, for Oñate also brought domestic animals to the Southwest.

Into a world that had no domestic animals except dogs and turkeys came 1,100 cattle, 4,000 sheep for wool and mutton, 1,000 goats, 150 colts, and 150 mares—animals supposedly reserved for the exclusive use of the Spaniards. However, with the Pueblo Revolt of 1680, the animals slipped into the possession of the indigenous people.

The Pueblos, particularly those along the Rio Grande, began to tend cattle, sheep, and goats along with crops.

The Navajos, meanwhile, embarked on a whole new way of life, becoming shepherds, but also, like other Apaches, horsemen, loving horses for the freedom and mobility the animals gave them.

SPIDER ROCK, CANYON DE CHELLY NATIONAL MIONUMENT, ARIZONA

The Navajos rapidly put aside any inclination to live in communities. Horses meant that they could freely wander the Southwest, and the Navajos soon discovered that the ownership of herd animals helped assure that the Diné could roam with little threat of hunger.

Soon, most Navajos were again living an at least semi-nomadic lifeway, following a pattern established by the grazing of their herds. They moved into the foothills of the towering San Juans or into the depths of the desert mountain ranges in summer to graze their animals, returning to the warmer, lower regions in winter.

In summer, if they built a dwelling at all, it was simply a branch-and-stick-covered square shelter with no walls—what the Spaniards called a *ramada*. In winter, they lived in hogans, circular structures built of stone and mud and later, especially after the arrival of steel tools to cut and shape the wood, out of wood beams arranged hexagonally, caulked with mud, and roofed with dirt.

Nonetheless, the Navajos did not abandon the cultivation of crops. Some grew crops near summer grazing areas, while those who adhered to more localized patterns of grazing for their animals cultivated crops near hogans in which they lived year around.

But horses also brought other changes.

Although made officially illegal by royal Spanish decree in 1532, slavery was an accepted institution throughout Spanish territories in the New World, due in part to the tremendous amount of work to be done to accomplish the Spaniards' goal of building a new empire, in part because of the shortage of people to do that work.

Although the Pueblos had represented an ideal source of slaves, as the Spanish empire expanded, even more people were needed to build cities and to work the enormous ranches of New Mexico and Mexico and the silver mines of Mexico.

Soon, Navajos and Utes of the Colorado Plateau; Comanches, a hunting-gathering, Shoshonean-speaking people of Colorado's and New Mexico's Great Plains; and Apaches of southern New Mexico and Arizona discovered a tremendous opportunity.

By the 1690s, using horses which allowed them to rapidly travel significant distances and to expeditiously ride into and out of various settlements, they were kidnapping other tribes' people at will. Annually, the horse-riding raiders gathered the people they had captured and took them to the Spanish settlement of Taos, New Mexico, to be sold as slaves, while the Spaniards rounded up every horse they could spare—the payment the horsemen coveted.

The Navajos also rapidly discovered that raids on other Indian communities and on Spanish ranches throughout New Mexico and northern Mexico gave them the opportunity to significantly expand their herds. Sheep, in particular, were taken by the hundreds, horses at every opportunity. After weeks of raiding, the Navajos commonly returned to the desert with thousands of animals, although it should be remembered that the Navajos were often similarly the victim of raids, especially at the hands of the nearby Utes.

Yet, the isolated, uncharted miles of their vast homeland helped protect them from reprisals. If pursued after a raid, the Navajos simply disappeared into their enormous domain. Early Spanish explorers despaired at the idea of entering those rugged, nearly impassable lands and simply labeled those places, *Tierra Incognito,* "Lands Unknown," on their maps and passed them by. The Navajos, confident that no one would follow them into the maze of canyons and high plateaus, raid-

ed with near impunity.

Thanks to the Spaniards' nearly insatiable appetite for slaves, horses helped bring anarchy to the Southwest—anarchy lasting nearly two hundred years until it was brought to a swift and terrible end by the United States.

The Long Walk

During the early 1860s, the United States government determined that the Navajo marauders must be subdued, in part to remove them from valuable lands.

Headed by explorer and Indian agent Col. Kit

HATALI YAZZIE, WARRIOR AND HEALER, CIRCA 1920

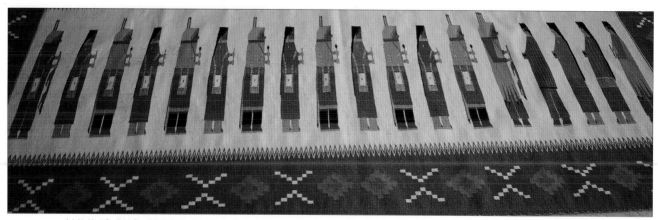

NAVAJO RUG, HUBBEL TRADING POST NATIONAL HISTORIC SITE, NAVAJO RESERVATION, ARIZONA

Carson, the New Mexico Volunteers were mustered during the Civil War to prevent pro-Confederate Arizona and Texas from giving aid to the Confederacy. The all-civilian regiment was also told to subdue the Navajos, as well as the Mescalero and Jicarilla Apaches of New Mexico's eastern plains.

Carson, whom the Navajos called "Red Shirt," knew that military force brought directly to bear against the Navajos would be useless. Rather than fight, they would simply fade into the remote back country until danger passed, a problem compounded by a lack of cohesive leadership

NAVAJO WOMAN IN TRADITIONAL DRESS

among the highly migratory people. The Navajos traveled in family groups or in dozens of loosely organized bands. While an agreement might be reached with one band to halt its raiding, others would merely continue.

Therefore, Carson and his troops killed every male Navajo they came across and set about methodically starving the remaining Navajos into submission.

They entered known Navajo strongholds, burning fields, destroying orchards, and either killing or taking Navajo livestock. Carson and his men, for example, spent seven days burning fields of corn and wheat at Canyon de Chelly, Arizona, a labyrinth of canyons carved as streams flowed from off the nearby Chuska Mountains to cut down into deposits of 200-million-year-old De Chelly Sandstone.

Carson placed a bounty on Navajo livestock captured by other indigenous people, an opportunity taken advantage of, in particular, by the Utes. He was willing to look the other way if citizens of the New Mexico and Arizona territories sold captured Navajos to Mexican slavers, though the United States was even then fighting a war against slavery.

Finally, by the spring of 1864, with most weakened by starvation, the Navajos began to straggle out of the desert to surrender. Many, however, escaped into the most remote regions of Navajo country: the isolated lands near Navajo Mountain in Utah, into the depths of the Grand Canyon, or across the San Juan River into the formidable canyons of southern Utah.

Those who surrendered were herded into corrals and detained at Fort Wingate, near Grants, New Mexico, or at Fort Defiance, Arizona, on the Arizona-New Mexico border southeast of Canyon de Chelly.

From here began what the Navajos consider to be one of the most infamous events in United States history, the "Long Walk."

In several large groups, the Navajos were herded more than three hundred miles across the desert to Fort Sumner, in extreme southeast New Mexico. Only the very old, the infirm, or the very young, were allowed to ride in wagons. Many, already weakened by hunger, died along the way.

But the real horror was they were being driven beyond the boundaries of Diné Bikéyah, their sacred homeland.

Long ago, when the Navajo gods climbed to the surface of this world from the world below, they carried with them earth taken from subterranean mountains of the previous world. This soil they piled at the four points of the compass, north, east, south, and west, respectively, to create the sacred mountains marking the outer edges of the Navajos' Diné Bikéyah.

At the southern edge of the La Plata range of the San Juan Mountains, towers the 13,000-foot heights of Hesperus Peak, Dibé Nitsaa, the northern most boundary of Diné Bikéyah. Meanwhile, along the eastern edge of the San Luis Valley in south-central Colorado, towers Mount Blanca, or

Sis Najiní. Jutting 14,000 feet into the Colorado sky, it represents the eastern-most edge of Diné Bikéyah.

Along the southern edge of the San Juan Basin towers Mount Taylor; the Navajos call it Dsoodzil. Its volcanic heights jut 11,389 feet from the flatness

NAVAJO WEAVER, HUBBELL TRADING POST NATIONAL HISTORICAL SITE, ARIZONA

of the New Mexico desert to form the southern boundary of Diné Bikéyah, while nearly three hundred miles due west of Mount Taylor, near Flagstaff, Arizona, rises Doo´k o oosliid, the 10,000-foot San Francisco Peaks, the western boundary of Diné Bikéyah.

As the Navajo were marched to Fort Sumner, they realized that they were being forced to go beyond the boundaries—formed by the sacred mountains—of their homeland. They believed that the sacred songs, such as the Blessingway, perhaps the oldest and most important of all Navajo

religious ceremonies, would no longer be effective. They felt wrenched from their land and their gods.

Finally, after a journey of weeks, the Navajos were herded into Fort Sumner, a prison camp beside the Little Pecos River. Here, at Bosque Redondo—Spanish for "Round Grove"—more than seven thousand Navajos and four hundred Mescalero Apaches were held prisoner for nearly five years. Hundreds died from malnutrition, disease, heat, and cold.

Eventually, after signing the Treaty of 1868, in which they agreed never to fight again, the Navajos were allowed to return home to live on a newly created reservation in their beloved redrock country of northeast Arizona, northwest New Mexico, and southeast Utah.

"When we saw the top of the (southern sacred) mountain from Albuquerque," recalled one Navajo leader of the return from Bosque Redondo, "we wondered if it was our mountain, and we felt like talking to the ground, we loved it so, and some of the old men and women cried with joy...."

The New Diné Bikéyah

At over sixteen million acres, the largest reservation in the United States, the Navajo reservation to which the Diné returned was nonetheless much smaller than Diné Bikéyah. Many could not in fact return to their homes, particularly in eastern Diné Bikéyah, near the Rio Grande in north-central New Mexico or in southwest Colorado.

And when the Navajos returned home, it was to more years of suffering. Their horses were gone, their herd animals were dead or gone, their fields were destroyed, and they lacked seeds with which to plant new crops.

For a time, the United States government, itself heavily burdened by the debt of the Civil War, agreed to provide them with provisions and later with new herd animals, but often the provisions did not arrive. The new livestock, meanwhile, were months in coming. Sometimes the Diné were reduced to eating rats to survive.

Officials hoped that ultimately the Navajos would support themselves solely by farming and animal husbandry in the tradition of the yeoman farmer, an idea probably formulated by those who had never seen the arid Colorado Plateau.

Somehow, the Navajos survived, and in 1869, fourteen thousand sheep and one thousand goats finally arrived—two animals for every man, woman, and child. Wrote the military commandant who distributed the animals to the Navajos, "I have never seen such anxiety and gratitude."

The Navajos often cared for and nurtured their new livestock while going hungry themselves, postponing butchering the animals so that the animals could multiply. All the Navajos took was a couple of pounds of wool per sheep at each shearing, wool carefully woven by the women into Navajo blankets, a skill their ancestors were taught by Pueblo men.

About the same time, Navajo men became silver artisans in earnest. A Navajo originally learned silversmithing from a New Mexican shortly before the Long Walk and then taught other Navajos. It was a craft for which Navajo artisans were eventually to become famous.

Both silver and blankets were subsequently traded for supplies at trading posts dotting the reservation, or better yet, for horses, the Navajos' ultimate symbol of wealth and esteem. The women owned and cared for the sheep; the men, the horses, all of which were rapidly increasing in number. By 1880, Navajo sheep numbered more than 700,000 animals.

Yet, there was still hardship ahead. Drought often killed crops or grasshoppers stripped both cultivated plants and wild forage needed by livestock. Sometimes winters brought crippling snow accumulations, causing animals and humans alike to starve.

Stock Reduction

But the Diné persevered, and by the turn of the century, their population had more than doubled, from roughly eight thousand when they left Bosque Redondo, to twenty thousand. Meanwhile, the sheep population increased to one million, goats to 250,000, horses to 100,500.

But by the 1920s and 1930s, that success brought new sadness to the Diné and greater hostility than anytime since the Long Walk.

The Navajo herds had simply multiplied until there were too many for the fragile desert of the Colorado Plateau. This was especially true since Navajos had been banished from the mountains and foothills in Colorado and along the eastern boundary of the traditional Diné Bikéyah in New Mexico. This largely ended the Navajos' centuries-old tradition of moving their animals into

the high country in the summer, therefore giving the desert a chance to rest and heal.

Beyond overgrazing, the sharp, cutting hooves of tens of thousands of sheep and goats compacted the soil and killed vegetation. And the animals suffered too. Beginning in the 1880s, sheep were smaller and produced less wool.

The effects of overgrazing can be seen to this day on the reservation.

Very old Navajos, staring off into the distance in nostalgic reverie, remember a land much different from the sunburned expanses of the present. They remember a green land, a fertile steppe filled with flowers and butterflies, a land carpeted with relatively rich growths of plant life. Now, however, there are only elusive glimpses of that land of

NAVAJO HERDER, MONUMENT VALLEY NAVAJO TRIBAL PARK, ARIZONA-UTAH

the past.

The busy highways cutting through the reservation have often been fenced to prevent livestock from wandering into traffic. Sometimes at the crest of a hill, where it is possible to see miles of highway stretched out distorted and shimmering in the distance, a great, long band of green snakes across the land within the fence line—a disturbing reminder of the Colorado Plateau landscape of just a few generations ago.

Therefore, in the 1930s, the United States government, vividly aware of erosion and the resulting Dust Bowl of the Great Plains, decided that the Navajo herds must be reduced. It launched what was to become the hated federal Navajo Livestock Reduction Program, which lasted through 1942.

The reservation was divided into grazing districts and the number of animals that each could realistically support was determined. The Navajos were then given quotas designating the number of animals they could own. Excess animals were sent to slaughter.

The Navajos were horrified at the loss of their animals. Financial compensation was of little value to a people who considered only animals to be a measure of wealth. Assurances that those which remained would be healthier were in vain.

Further bitterness was sown with the tactless decision to sometimes allow white ranchers to graze their livestock on areas of the reservation where Navajo livestock numbers were being reduced. The Navajos were also enraged when 3,500 goats were shot and left to rot in the desert sun, a cheap alternative to sending them to distant slaughterhouses. Such waste and disregard for life deeply offended the Diné.

Sometimes stock reduction went to even greater extremes. So many Navajo churro sheep—an especially hardy breed known for its two-textured wool—were killed that the breed still teeters on the brink of extinction.

In spite of the heartbreak of stock reduction, most of the reservation continues to be overgrazed, contributing to depleted plant life and to the spread of desertification. Some areas are currently grazed by eight times as many animals as the land can realistically carry.

Yet, despite the bitterness caused by stock reduction, Navajo soldiers enlisted in the military and may have well helped turn the tide of World

NAVAJO ARTISAN, LILY HOLIDAY

War II in the Pacific theater. The now-famous Navajo "Code Talkers" communicated strategic information in the Navajo language, confounding the Japanese, who thought they were dealing with a new form of code. Ironically, at the same time, Navajo children were being punished for speaking Navajo at the government-operated boarding schools they were required to attend on and off the reservation.

Today, even though many Navajos are college educated, poverty continues to be a major problem for a reservation population estimated at about 200,000. The Navajos also have a high birth rate, at 2.8 per couple, roughly equal to that in many developing nations—and, like many developing nations, in a land severely lacking in many essential natural resources, especially water.

Despite construction of some of the world's largest power plants, owned by off-reservation interests and generating electricity for Los Angeles, San Diego, Phoenix, Albuquerque, and Tucson; despite the power plants' accompanying coal strip mines, which annually remove thousands of tons of coal; despite a controversial timber operation in the Chuska Mountains and construction of an enormous water project and associated agribusiness near Farmington, New Mexico, as well as employment for many in Navajo tribal government and tourist-oriented operations, high unemployment continues to be a pervasive problem on the reservation.

Meanwhile, environmental damage from strip mining, wells depleted by the removal of ground water for energy production, and air pollution from power generation are the *de facto* legacy of energy production, while there is growing criticism that timber operations are harvesting the tribe's limited timber resources beyond sustainable levels.

Yet, Navajo tradition survives. A few hogans and ramadas still dot the desert. Some Navajos still live very much as their ancestors did before them, often in regions so isolated that they are rarely visited by outsiders. Many still speak only Navajo and live nearly independent of a cash economy, surviving off the crops they grow, the animals they raise, and the money they make crafting silver or weaving blankets, which some Navajos increasingly sell at commercial outlets, or astutely, directly to visitors to the reservation.

SUN AND EARTH

The Navajos do not embrace the concept of life after death, believing instead that when an individual dies, while some corrupt ghostly remnants of his character may linger, he or she basically ceases to exist.

In life, Navajos use a complicated series of songs, chants, prayers, and herbal medicines to stay in harmony with the natural forces of the universe or to bend those forces to their benefit.

Like the Pueblo people, the Navajos believe that everything has a spiritual essence. Moreover, that which nurtures and gives life to all things—Mother Earth—is a living, sentient being fostered in her work by the power of Father Sun or Father Sky. To the Navajos, everything in nature is male or female, even the rain.

Perhaps this belief system reflects a culture where equality between the sexes is deeply ingrained. Clan lines, for example, run from one generation to the next through the woman's side of the family. A Navajo man is of his mother's clan, while Navajo women retain their names and family identity after marriage and control much of the family property, which is in turn inherited by their female descendents.

Meanwhile, in Navajo religion, the rainbow is the path of the Yei, "The Holy Ones," the offspring of Mother Earth and Father Sky. The Yei, incidentally, may be either good or evil and, like the Pueblo kachinas, are impersonated during at least some important religious ceremonies.

The Navajo religion is a study in striving for harmony and a rapport between humankind and nature. All things in nature are believed to have powers, as reflected in certain traits of their being. The sun, moon, thunder, and water represent the power of motion; rocks, plants, and earth represent endurance and rejuvenation; and the coyote represents cunning. It is the Navajos' task to evoke these powers to their benefit using elaborate chants.

Humans exist on an equal plane with all other creatures and things.

Similarly, there is no god of absolute power or authority. While Father Sun may be considered to be a high god, without Changing Woman, who represents the changing seasons, and Mother Earth, he is powerless.

When a chant is needed, a visionary, a listener, a hand trembler, or a star gazer—one who has the ability to hear or to see revelations—determines which chant is appropriate for a given set of circumstances. If someone is ill, different variations of religious ceremonies must be performed according to the type of illness. Those who become ill while around non-Navajos, for example, require the chanting of the Enemy Way. In each ceremony, the powers of the four sacred

NAVAJO SANDPAINTER

border mountains, as well as other sacred mountains and their deities, are invoked.

Each sacred chant, of which there are more than fifty, has been passed down verbally in meticulous detail for generations. These ceremonies, some lasting days, with their accompanying "great mass of intricate ritual," as Western photographer and historian Laura Gilpin called it, must be performed in exact detail, for it is believed that "sings" were given to the Navajos directly by the gods.

Most chants are accompanied by specific sandpaintings, intricate geometric designs meticulously created with colored sands, pollens, seeds, vegetable matter, meal, and minerals according to a pre-established pattern. On these, the gods are depicted, probably more than coincidentally, looking like the masked kachinas of the Pueblos.

Close to the conclusion of the sing, the person for whom it is being held, sits on the completed sandpainting and is believed to literally take on the powers of the supernatural forces depicted in it. He or she is cautioned not to touch others for fear of harming them.

At the conclusion of the ceremony, he or she removes the supernatural powers by bathing in sacred yucca soap, and then acknowledges what the gods have done for him or her by arising early to "breathe in" the dawn. Finally, each sandpainting, although elaborate and beautiful, is disassembled in the reverse order of its creation to prevent any modification by witches in a way that might cause evil.

65

AUTUMN SCRUB OAKS, CONTINENTAL DIVIDE, JICARILLA APACHE RESERVATION, NEW MEXICO

The Jicarilla Apaches

While the Apachu de Navajo dispersed across the Colorado Plateau, most other Apaches traveled into lands to the south to make their homes.

The Lipan Apaches settled in eastern New Mexico and western Texas, eventually moving into Mexico under pressure from the Comanches. The Mescalero Apaches, named after their love of eating the tender meat of the mescal, or agave, cactus, lived in south-central New Mexico near the Sacramento Mountains. The Mimbrenos lived along the Mimbres River in western New Mexico and were closely allied with the Chiricahua Apaches, who lived in the Chiricahua Mountains of southeast Arizona, in the Sierra Madres in Chihuahua, Mexico, and in southwest New Mexico.

The Western Apaches, meanwhile, consisted of the White Mountain Apaches, living along the southern rim of the Colorado Plateau in Arizona, and the Cibecue and San Carlos tribes, living slightly further south. The Western Apaches, were linguistically and culturally the most closely related to the Navajos, probably having separated from them only in the relatively recent past.

Undoubtedly the raiding tradition which brought tragedy to the Navajos also brought tragedy to the Apaches, particularly the Chiricahuas, to the south of the Colorado Plateau.

The Mexican state of Chihuahua placed a bounty on the scalps of all Apache men, women, and children in 1837. This led to the slaughter not

66

only of Apaches but of other Indians, even Mexicans, as bounty hunters harvested any scalp that might pass for that of an Apache.

When the United States won its war with Mexico and assumed Mexican lands in the Southwest, the Apaches were delighted to be free of Mexican domination and felt admiration for those who had driven the Mexicans out—a friendship that ended quickly and bitterly with the discovery of gold and silver on Apache lands.

As American settlers and miners moved into the Arizona and New Mexico territories, they intruded upon Apache lands and demanded that the Apaches be removed. In 1871, a group of citizens from Tucson, Arizona, allied with Hispanics and nearby Papago Indians—or Tohono o'otam, as they prefer to be called—historic enemies of the Apaches, attacked an Apache encampment while the Apache men were away hunting. Upwards of 140 Apaches

JICARILLA APACHE WARRIORS; DATE, NAMES UNKNOWN
COURTESY: COLORADO HISTORICAL SOCIETY

were murdered, all but eight of them women or children. President Grant demanded that the perpetrators be tried; however, after deliberating less than thirty minutes, a Tucson jury found the defendants not guilty of all charges.

Apaches soon were forced onto reservations, which were too small and too inhospitable for self-sufficiency, forcing them to depend upon the government for supplies which were often inedible or inadequate.

The seeds of strife were sown.

Cochise and Geranimo

The Chiricahuas, in particular, suffered. They were placed on the San Carlos Indian Reservation in central Arizona, to the south of the Colorado Plateau, where temperatures frequently climbed above 120 degrees Fahrenheit. A military outpost there had earlier been abandoned because of outbreaks of malaria among the soldiers.

Apache children, in particular, suffered and died. Some historians feel the Apaches' placement at San Carlos was a deliberate attempt at extermination.

Ultimately, the Chiricahuas decided they had to flee the reservation or die. But when they escaped and resumed their old raiding life, the outcry from Americans was loud and frenzied. A Tucson newspaper, for example, called for attacks on the Apaches, "...until every valley and crest and crag and fastness shall send to high heaven the grateful incense of festering and rotting Chiricahuas."

Called by some the finest warriors North America ever saw, the Chiricahuas, led first by Cochise and then by Geronimo after Cochise's death in 1874, conducted a long and successful war against the United State and Mexico.

Geronimo was not a hereditary chief, but in the democratic Apache tradition, had earned the right to lead based on his skills as a hunter and warrior. Also, like most Apache leaders, he was a spiritualist, who reportedly had psychic powers.

Numbering only about twelve hundred people, the Chiricahuas hid in the Chiricahua Mountains and the Sierra Madres and conducted a campaign of guerilla warfare, a last, desperate bid for freedom and dignity. Borne of their hatred of whites, they left a trail of blood across northern Mexico and the Arizona and New Mexico territories.

Geronimo's own stake in the conflict was not small; his mother, wife, and three small children were murdered by Sonoran soldiers during a massacre of an Apache encampment near the town of Janos, Mexico, in 1850. He considered the attack cowardly since the soldiers had attacked only after ascertaining that no Apache warriors were in the area.

By the 1880s, thousands of Mexican troops and five thousand United States soldiers, almost a quarter of the Army, were told to crush the last handful of Chiricahuas. Ultimately, much of Geronimo's band was captured at its stronghold in the remote depths of the Sierra Madres, while Geronimo and his warriors were miles away.

Tradition has it that spiritualist Geronimo had a vision of the capture of his people as it happened. He surrendered of his own accord some months later. Despite his repeated pleas to be allowed to return home to die, he eventually died at Fort Sill, Oklahoma, after first enduring a prolonged exile in a Florida concentration camp.

The Apache de la Xicarilla

Apache de la Xicarilla, "The People of the Baskets" or "Little Basket Makers," as the Spaniards called them, were named for the skill for which they are still known.

The Xicarilla, or Jicarilla, ranged a homeland they believed was given them by Black Hac ´c't cin, the "Creator," the omnipotent source of all supernatural power. That traditional homeland, although including much of southwest Colorado's San Juan Mountains, rested for the most part beyond the boundaries of the Colorado Plateau. It also included the Sangre de Cristo Mountains of southern Colorado and northern New Mexico and the Jemez and Sandia mountains of north-central New Mexico. From there, it extended east across the Colorado and New Mexico plains to what is now Oklahoma.

Originally two distinct groups, the Olleros, the "Mountain People," and the Llanero, the "Plains People," the Jicarillas, who collectively called themselves the Tindé, the "People," were heavily influenced by the cultures of the Great Plains and the Pueblos. Like the people of the plains, they wore deerskin moccasins, lived in tepees made of animal skins sewn together and stretched over a frame of wooden poles. They dressed in buckskin and were hunter-gatherers. All were extraordinary equestrians, with girls, like boys, taught to capture, tame, and ride horses, and to shoot bows and arrows.

The Jicarilla women did most of the gathering and were knowledgeable of an amazingly wide range of plants: which could be eaten, where they could be gathered, when they could be harvested, the medicinal qualities of each, and the non-food uses to which they could be put. The men hunted, traveling far onto the plains to kill buffalo and antelope and into the mountains for deer, elk, and mountain sheep.

The western Jicarillas, the Olleros, or "Mountain People," had, like the Navajos, been heavily influenced by the Pueblos in the development of agriculture, in some instances going so far as to abandon their tepees in favor of pueblo-type houses. Eventually, the Llanero of the plains also learned to practice horticulture to supplement the natural harvest of plants and animals.

The religion of Jicarillas, like that of the Navajos, was probably heavily influenced by the Pueblos. All three religions embrace the idea of humans emerging to the surface of this world from a world below, while the Jicarillas, like many of the Pueblos, participate even today in an annual sacred race.

The Olleros, representing the sun and the animals, and the Llaneros, representing the moon and plants, meet in September for three days of religious preparation. Two kiva-like structures are built, one at each end of a race track, and sacred sandpaintings are made in concert with the recitation of sacred chants. If representatives of the Olleros win the race, it signifies that wild game will be abundant during the coming year, a Llaneros victory signifies that plants will be abundant.

The Jicarillas, like the Pueblos and the Navajos, also observe puberty rites.

The arrival of the horse into the Jicarillas' lifeway, as in the instance of the Navajos and other Apaches, meant the addition of raiding to their culture, particularly against other plains-area peoples. Beyond that, the Jicarillas traded heavily with the Pueblos, who in the earlier years may have encouraged them and other Apaches to live nearby to help defend against the Spaniards.

The Colorado Plateau

When Jicarilla lands were part of the Mexican frontier, isolation and a comparative lack of resources attracted little attention to the Jicarillas. However, when their homeland became part of the United States, a wholesale influx of settlers began.

The Jicarillas found themselves pushed from their traditional lands and deprived of their livelihood. As they tried to become

CARSON NATIONAL FOREST, NEW MEXICO

more dependent upon agriculture, drought repeatedly killed their crops. Facing the possibility of starvation, they stepped up raids for cattle. But as more settlers arrived and hostilities increased, the Jicarillas finally had to turn to the government for food rations.

Acting Governor William S. Messervy of the New Mexico Territory stated in 1854 that "...the best interests of this territory and the highest dictates of humanity demanded their (the Jicarillas') extinction."

By that time, the Jicarillas were begging that a reservation be set aside for them, a proposal to which many New Mexicans

YOUNG JICARILLA HORSEWOMAN, TEPEE IN BACKGROUND
PHOTOGRAPH: STEPHEN TRIMBLE

were opposed, in part because they profited economically from the presence of the military and the large number of troops required to keep peace in the region. Each time a new area was targeted as potential reservation, some New Mexicans launched either real or fictitious claims to the land. In another instance, a proposal for a reservation in Colorado's San Juan Mountains was terminated when gold was discovered there.

The Jicarillas ultimately were ordered to at least temporarily join the Mescalero Apaches on a reservation in southern New Mexico. After a comparatively short time, however, the Jicarillas, homesick for northern New Mexico and frustrated by their inability to grow crops with water which was too alkaline, quietly went home and refused to return to the reservation even when ordered to do so.

Finally, at the urging of the Ute chief, Ouray, the half-brother of a Jicarilla leader, a Jicarilla delegation traveled to Washington, D.C., to directly ask President Grover Cleveland to establish a reservation for them, a request supported by a military eager to have squabbles between Anglos and the Jicarillas resolved. A reservation in the piñon- and pine-studded foothills of the San Juan Mountains in extreme northern New Mexico and along the eastern edge of the San Juan Basin was established by executive order in 1887.

It was mostly through the formation of this reservation that the Jicarilla Apaches moved to the extreme eastern edge of the Colorado Plateau, on lands adjoining the Navajo reservation—near but not including most of the Jicarillas' original homeland.

The Suffering Continues

Even with the establishment of the reservation, the Jicarillas' suffering was far from over.

White settlers intruded onto the reservation,

taking the best lands and leaving the Jicarillas lands lacking water or at elevations too high for agriculture. And while timber from the reservation was being sold by the government and the profits deposited in the United States treasury in non-interest-bearing accounts, the Jicarillas starved. Meanwhile, the entire southern half of the reservation was leased by the government to whites for livestock grazing.

The malnourished, poverty-stricken people were ravaged by disease. Tuberculosis, measles, trachoma—which caused blindness—and influenza took their toll. From 824 people in 1891, the Jicarilla population plummeted to 588 by 1920. Health problems were compounded by the Jicarillas' years-long fight for educational facilities for their children. When schools were finally built, disease spread from the schools outward into the community, often because of mismanagement. One public health official discovered, for example, that drinking water at one school was muddy and contained dead mice.

Not until the 1930s, and the passage of the Indian Reorganization Act, did the Jicarillas' lot improve. That act worked to remove those who had intruded onto the reservation and to consolidate Indian holdings. It also moved the government away from a paternalistic attitude, and for the first time recognized the full rights of citizenship for Indians under the Constitution. As Indians, including the Jicarillas, began to have control over their own resources, their lot improved, although years of poverty left a deep, perhaps indelible, mark on them.

Today, the lives of the roughly three thousand Jicarillas are improving. The tribe derives significant income from the operation of a tribal-owned casino at Dulce, New Mexico, and from selling permits to hunt and fish on their still largely undeveloped lands.

THE PAI

The Grand Canyon. Beyond a doubt the most stupendous canyon on Earth, it is a mile deep, phenomenally beautiful, unbelievably rugged, so immense as to almost defy comprehension.

Amazingly, humankind has lived in and around that craggy chasm for thousands of years.

People of the Paleo-Indian culture hunted in Grand Canyon, where the Anasazi apparently remained until about 1200 A.D. That is when the Grand Canyon area, like many other regions of the Colorado Plateau, experienced a mass exodus of the Anasazi.

The Cohonina culture was somewhat similar to that of the Basketmaker, although much simpler.

HAVASUPAI WOMAN WITH CHILD IN BURDEN BASKET, CIRCA 1870
COURTESY: U.S. DEPARTMENT OF THE INTERIOR, GRAND CANYON NATIONAL PARK, IDENTIFICATION NUMBER 5117

the area around eleven thousand years ago, while people of the Desert Archaic culture were probably in the area beginning about seven thousand years ago. "Split-twig" figurines, representing deer, antelope, and bighorn sheep, have been found stashed in caves in the canyon, probably religious fetishes left there by wandering hunters ten thousand to twelve thousand years ago.

But beginning about three thousand years ago, people seem to have abandoned the Grand Canyon area, until about 600 A.D. when the Cohonina people of the Desert Archaic tradition began to settle on the Coconino Plateau along the South Rim of the canyon.

About the same time, the Basketmaker Anasazi moved onto the North Rim. Over two thousand Anasazi cultural sites have been found at the

The Cohonina lived in unadorned stone or wood houses for part of the year, and they had no kivas or other religious structures. By about 900 A.D., pressures from the thriving Anasazi culture may have forced them to move to the west end of the Coconino Plateau, where their culture died out, perhaps absorbed by surrounding peoples, perhaps forced from the region entirely.

By about 1050 A.D., the Cerbat Indians—likely the ancestors of today's Pai people—moved into the Grand Canyon from the south and west.

Presently, there are three major groups of Pai people, the Havasupai, living at the bottom of the

MATHER POINT, SOUTH RIM,
GRAND CANYON NATIONAL PARK, ARIZONA

71

SUPAI VILLAGE, GRAND CANYON, ARIZONA

Grand Canyon; the Hualapai (also spelled Walapai), living immediately south of the west end of the Grand Canyon; and the historic enemies of both peoples, the Yavapai, living beyond the boundaries of the Colorado Plateau to the south of the Bill Williams River in west-central Arizona.

The Havasupai and Hualapai, each consisting of several bands, thought of themselves as being of the same tribe—the "Only True People on Earth"—until the 1860s. But then, they were forced onto two different reservations by the United States government, which classified them separately and at least legally split them.

All speak the Yuman language, indigenous to the Colorado River region of southwest Arizona, extreme southern California, and northwest Mexico.

The Desert Culture

Before the 1860s, the Colorado Plateau Pai people consisted of a dozen or so bands living south of and in the Grand Canyon, pursuing a lifeway that was one of the strongest surviving examples of the Desert Archaic tradition.

The Pai practiced a modified seasonal round, moving to the river bottoms and protected canyons to plant crops during the summer and then scattering across the countryside in winter to hunt and gather. Each band had a specific area to which it laid claim, and each was known by a name descriptive of the place where the band spent most of the seasonal round.

The Havasupai were known as the "People of the Blue-Green Water," after the color of the water of Havasu Creek, as it flows toward the Colorado River just below that river's confluence with the Little Colorado.

There, in the depths of the Grand Canyon, in a place that American explorer Frank H. Cushing in 1881 called, "a veritable land of summer," the Havasupai raised corn, beans, squash, peaches, apricots, cotton, tobacco, and sunflowers—crops irrigated with the waters of Havasu Creek.

Some bands of the Hualapai or "Pine Springs People," practiced agriculture in the western extremes of the Grand Canyon, while still others cultivated crops along the Colorado River below the canyon. These lands were part of the greater Pai's traditional realm, a land which they believed had been set aside for them by divine intercession.

The Pai homeland stretched from the east shore of the Colorado River, as it turns south toward Mexico after leaving the Grand Canyon, east along the Bill Williams River, and then across the Coconino Plateau to the distant San Francisco Peaks. Hindered by the region's dry climate, some bands farmed only sporadically and were largely dependent upon hunting and gathering, although they sometimes also traded sea shells—acquired from California and Mexico—with the Hopis for needed goods.

During the more settled months of their semi-sedentary existence, the Pai lived in loosely organized villages near their gardens. The Pai's houses were dome-shaped huts made of poles, bark, and branches; small square-shaped dwellings made of poles and brush; or small, square- or rectangular-shaped stone structures.

Each band was led by a headman, who had little authority and who had to lead by persuasion or by simply earning the respect of his followers. In the Pai's unstructured existence, little tribal authority or influence was wanted or permitted. While the eligibility to be a headman was inherited, the actual right to lead was granted based on ability or the wishes of a previous headman.

Like many other people of the Colorado Plateau, the Havasupai and Hualapai adopted elements of the Pueblo religion, specifically masked dancing, rain dances, and prayer sticks for prayers to the sun, Earth, water, and rocks. They believed in life after death and in ghosts, and they believed in the ability of spiritual leaders—shamans—to cure diseases and injuries and to influence the weather. Historically, the Pai cremated their dead, all of the possessions of the dead, and annually burned food, clothing, and other possessions to honor the dead and provide for them in the afterlife.

Gold and Tragedy

Contact with outsiders in the rugged, isolated lands of northern Arizona was minimal until gold was discovered on Pai lands in the Hualapai and Cerbat mountains in 1865—the beginning of the end for an age-old way.

Miners soon swarmed across Pai lands, blocking access to critical hunting, gathering, and planting areas. The miners were followed by cattlemen, who often denied the Pai access to the sparse scattering of springs and watering holes or whose animals fouled water supplies or destroyed crops.

Some of the Pai began to exchange woven goods, acquired from the Pueblos, with the Mohave people of southern Arizona for horses and weapons. Finally, after months of increasing tension, Hualapai chief Wauba Yuma was killed by prospectors, triggering the Hualapai Wars of the 1860s.

But by the late 1860s, the Hualapai and their southern Arizona kin, the Yavapai, had been defeated and faced a tragic one-year internment at La Paz on the lower Colorado River. Many of them, accustomed to the cooler temperatures on the high plateau near the Grand Canyon, died from the stifling heat. Although they were finally allowed to leave La Paz, not until 1883 was a reservation formally established for them near the edge of the Grand Canyon near Peach Springs, Arizona, on lands only a fraction of the size of their original domain.

The Havasupai, meanwhile, avoided confrontation, instead withdrawing into the isolation of the Grand Canyon. There, in the 1880s, out of their original enormous homeland, they were granted 518 acres as a reservation.

Meanwhile, the use of both the Hualapai's and Havasupai's historic lands used for hunting and gathering was curtailed, bringing the seasonal round to an abrupt end and subjecting them to complete destitution and dependence on government handouts. Poverty and disease nearly decimated both. In 1881, for example, there were an estimated 214 Havasupai, but by 1890 that had dropped to 166.

Today, the combined Havasupai, Hualapai, and Yavapai populations total roughly two thousand people.

LEE MARSHALL, HAVASUPAI ELDER, SUPAI, ARIZONA
PHOTOGRAPH: STEPHEN TRIMBLE

The Hualapai economy is based on livestock, timber harvesting, and limited farming, and the number who can live on the reservation is severely restricted by a lack of economic opportunities.

The Havasupai, who until recent years still lived in traditional thatch houses in the eight-hundred-year-old village of Supai at the bottom of the Grand Canyon, now live mostly in government-issue prefabricated houses—flown into the canyon by helicopter. The Havasupai continue to farm and raise orchards on small plots just upstream from four beautiful waterfalls—including Mooney Falls, at 196 feet, higher than Niagara Falls—formed as Havasu Creek travels along a narrow gorge leading toward the bottom of the Grand Canyon.

Supplies arrive via U.S. Mail, brought to the canyon rim along Indian Route 18 from Peach Springs, Arizona, and then into the canyon on mule or horseback along the same rugged trail that has been the only access to the village for centuries—the last mail route in the nation still delivered by pack train.

The Havasupai encourage limited tourism at the tribal-owned Havasupai Lodge in the Grand Canyon, although the number of visitors is restricted in the interest of preserving the Havasupai culture and the fragile canyon-bottom environment.

One profound concern of the villagers is that thousands of mining claims, most for uranium, exist within the greater Supai watershed—mining held at bay only because the world uranium market is glutted.

The tiny village historically has fallen frequent victim to flash floods, caused when heavy thunderstorms send water and boulders crashing down the steep walls of the canyon and into the village.

The Southern Paiutes

In the not so distant past, the Southern Paiutes traveled the western-most extremes of the Colorado Plateau, like the Pai people, living a nearly intact form of the Desert Archaic culture in lands in and near the spectacularly beautiful Zion and Bryce canyon regions of southwest Utah and deep into the Arizona Strip, that portion of Arizona north of the Grand Canyon.

Their simple hunter-gatherer existence was aptly suited to the beautiful but extremely harsh lands upon which they lived. Southern Paiutes traveled in small, mobile family groups, so that they would not demand too much of any one place for too long. They hunted with bows made of chokecherry bush limbs wrapped in sinew affixed with glue derived by boiling the hooves of recently killed animals. Arrow tips were dipped into poison to expedite the kill.

The tribe had shamans believed to have healing powers and who it was thought influenced the weather. Each gained his supernatural powers in a dream or vision, and each specialized in treating a particular kind of illness. The Paiutes, more than attributing special powers to shamans directly, believed that they were an instrument through which the Creator, or Ahppu, worked.

The Paiutes, a term of unknown origins which may mean, "True Utes," lived mostly in temporary brush shelters erected along their routes of travel, although often in summer no shelters were used at all. They made simple brown to reddish-brown pottery, with cone-shaped bottoms, and wove burden baskets, hats, and coiled baskets out of native plants. Their simple, migratory lifestyle left little need for structured religious or social organization, and leadership, what little was needed, was determined not by heredity but by an individual's ability to convince others that he was worthy of being a leader.

The Paiutes affixed often colorful and descriptive names to the features of the Colorado Plateau landscape. They, for example, named the Zion Canyon cul-de-sac, Loogoon, "Arrow Quiver," or "Leave the Way You Entered," and

PAIUTE WOMEN
1871-1872 POWELL EXPEDITION
COURTESY: COLORADO HISTORICAL SOCIETY

Bryce Canyon with its thousands of strangely shaped "hoodoo" rock formations, Unka-timpe-wa-wince-pock-ich, "Red Rocks Standing Like People in a Bowl-Shaped Canyon."

They ate prairie dogs, ground squirrels, rabbits, fish—a dietary taboo of the Apaches and Navajos—deer, antelope, elk, piñon nuts, grass seeds, and some forms of insects and insect larvae, a practice that was to later earn them the contemptuous nickname, "Digger Indians," from American settlers. Nonetheless, the Paiute learned to survive, even to thrive, on a land where several Spanish exploration parties nearly starved.

The Southern Paiutes were part of the much larger Paiute tribe, who spoke a Shoshonean dialect of the Uto-Aztecan language and who in prehistory lived in the Great Basin region of southern California, southeast Oregon, southwest Idaho, northwest Utah, and throughout Nevada.

Linguistically, they were closely related to other Shoshonean-speaking people, including the Utes of Utah and Colorado; the Comanches of the Great Plains; the Hopis of northern Arizona; the Papagos of south-central Arizona; the Pimas of southern Arizona and northern Mexico; the Shoshones of California, Nevada, and Idaho; and the Tarahumaras and Nahuatls of Mexico. The Uto-Aztecan language was, in other words, spoken from Idaho to the Isthmus of Tehuantepec and from the Great Plains to the Pacific.

The Southern Paiutes may have been descendents of the mysterious Fremont people, who lived upon the Colorado Plateau fifteen hundred years ago, or they may have moved into the northern areas of the Southwest from the Great Basin around 1000 A.D. The Southern Paiutes' ancestors apparently lived peacefully alongside the Anasazi until competition for limited resources may have caused discord and may have contributed to the Anasazi exodus.

The Anasazi may have taught the Paiutes their

PREVIOUS PAGE: TAYLOR CREEK,
ZION NATIONAL PARK, UTAH

first agricultural skills, triggering a change in Paiute lifestyle from totally hunting and gathering to semi-sedentary. The Paiutes became agricultural to the extent that they learned to plant crops in the spring and return to harvest them in the fall.

The Strangers Arrive

Historically, Paiute lands were mostly ignored by Spain and Mexico, and with the exception of some Paiutes captured and sold as slaves, the Paiutes remained largely free of harassment by Spaniards and Mexicans.

The entry of American settlers, however, brought extreme hardship, in part because of the Americans' ignorance of how to live upon the harsh, fragile lands of the Colorado Plateau.

As Mormon settlers poured into Utah and settlers and miners traveled through Utah to reach California, their livestock and horses competed with wild game for sparse grazing, and the settlers killed game animals, radically reducing game populations and upsetting the balance which had allowed the Paiutes to survive on marginal lands. Meanwhile, as Mormon ranchers fanned across Utah and northern Arizona, they demanded the greenest valleys with the most—sometimes the only—dependable water, shutting the Southern Paiutes from areas where they had grown crops for generations.

THE WATCHMAN, ZION NATIONAL PARK, UTAH

Fortunately, much of the violence Indians faced elsewhere from settlers was tempered by Mormon leader Brigham Young's admonition to his people, "It is better to feed them (the Paiutes) than to fight them," and his desire to forge an alliance with his Paiute neighbors. This not only prevented bloodshed, but gave the Paiutes a place to turn for help as they began to lose their self-sufficiency and face hunger.

The Mormons were eager to teach the Paiutes new agricultural methods. The Paiutes, seeing the Mormons' enormous harvests, in some instances, actually sought the opportunity to live near them in order to learn. Others, however, fled to live among the Northern Paiutes to distance themselves from Mormon proselytizing.

Settlers sometimes also unwittingly brought catastrophe to the Paiutes. In one instance near Kanab, Utah, for example, after contact with set-

tlers, one hundred Southern Paiutes died of measles, a devastating toll for a people numbering only a thousand or so.

By 1855, tensions between settlers and the Paiutes became critical, as a massive drought killed most of the crop of grass seed, a staple of the Paiute diet, already in shortage with the loss of traditional hunting and farming lands. In an attempt to protect native grasses and as an alternative food source, the Paiutes killed ever more of the settlers' livestock. They also attacked settlers as they passed through the region in an attempt to frighten them away and to take food, supplies, and livestock from them.

It was in that atmosphere the Paiutes were accused of the Mountain Meadows Massacre, in what is now the Dixie National Forest about twenty-five miles northwest of Saint George, Utah. A wagon train of non-Mormon settlers traveling through southwest Utah in 1857 was attacked and all occupants, except a few babies or very small children, were murdered.

But history later revealed that while the Paiutes may have played a part in earlier harassing and attacking the wagon train, it was actually Mormons who committed the final, deadly attack.

The Mormons had fled to Utah, then part of Mexico, in the 1840s—calling it the promised land of Deseret, or "Beehive"—after years of religious persecution, including the murder by a mob in 1844 of Mormon prophet and founder Joseph Smith in Carthage, Missouri, and the burning of the Mormon city of Nauvoo, Illinois.

But with the end of the United States' war with Mexico, Utah became United States territory, and anti-Mormon sentiment continued—largely because of the Mormon practice of polygamy. At the same time, great influxes of settlers and miners were heading to California through Utah, increasing the Mormons' fears that the persecution they had escaped would merely follow them to Utah.

Mormon leader Brigham Young, vowing the Mormons would never again fall victim, especially in their own Deseret, established an army of Mormon volunteers and made no secret of his hatred of Americans. As tensions mounted, President Buchanan in 1856 ordered troops to the

Utah Territory.

It appeared there would be war, although the troops encountered a harsh winter during their long journey across the frontier and never arrived. Young, meanwhile, was stripped by the United States of his authority as territorial governor in mid-1857.

By September, a time when anti-American sentiment had reached a fever pitch, the wagon train from Arkansas—en route to California—arrived in Utah to be attacked by a Mormon militia as the wagon train approached Saint George.

For years, the Mormons claimed their militia came upon the wagon train only after a massacre by Paiutes, but the truth began to leak out, and in 1877, Brigham Young's son, John Lee —who established Lee's Ferry on the Colorado River—was executed for his part in the massacre, bitterly claiming that he had been made a scapegoat for a deed in which many other Mormons had played a part.

ELVA DRYE, SOUTHERN PAIUTE ELDER
PHOTOGRAPH: STEPHEN TRIMBLE

The Paiutes, meanwhile, learned from the Plains Indians that more settlers were headed west "like Locusts" and that fighting the onslaught was futile.

In 1873, famous Western explorer, John Wesley Powell wrote of the Southern Paiutes, "They fully understand that the settlement of the country by white men is inevitable...Their hunting-grounds have been spoiled, their favorite valleys are occupied by white men, and they are compelled to scatter in small bands in order to obtain sustenance."

Dance of Hope

It was during these times that the Ghost Dance came to the Southern Paiutes and many other tribes of the West and Great Plains. In 1869, a Northern Paiute mystic by the name of Wodziwob claimed to have had a vision in which the old Anglo-dominated world ended. Afterward, dead Indians, along with the buffalo, returned to a world that was again free, fertile, and nurturing.

For this vision to come true, he instructed his followers to sing certain songs, perform ritual dances, and wear symbolic costumes, creating a movement that spread like wildfire among the indigenous people of the West.

When the rituals did not work, the movement lost momentum. However, with the continuing Indian tragedies in the 1880s, the Ghost Dance experienced a resurgence under another Northern Paiute, Wovoka. Some Indians, particularly the Sioux of the Great Plains, even believed that if they wore "ghost shirts," supposedly impervious to bullets, they would be protected from injury.

Apprehension about the movement caused the government to direct the military to bring a halt to Ghost Dances, leading to eventual tragedy when over three hundred Sioux, including women and children, were massacred by the Army at Wounded Knee, South Dakota, as they gathered for a Ghost Dance.

With that tragedy, the last hope of resuming the old ways died.

Soon, in a tragic repetition of a regrettable pattern, the Southern Paiutes were relegated to reservations. In the poverty and filth in which they were forced to live, illness took a major toll. In the 1920s, for example, the Southern Paiutes' Northern Paiute kin on the Pyramid Lake reservation in Nevada suffered from active tuberculosis at a rate of 327 per one thousand people, the highest of any Indians and many times higher than among non-Indians.

In a baffling decision, the government in the 1950s declared the Shivwits Paiute incapable of handling the affairs of a reservation and ordered a Utah bank to sell off all reservation lands. However, the property was so poor and so lacking in water that no buyer was ever found.

The Shivwits Paiute, meanwhile, uneducated and cut off from government benefits, entered abject, total poverty, carving out a pathetic existence on the fringes of communities in southern Utah and northern Arizona. Later, the Shivwits reservation was reinstated.

Like many Indians, the Southern Paiutes benefited from monies gained under the Indian Claims Act of 1946. They were finally compensated in the 1970s for lands taken from them during the nineteenth century, revenues which allowed the tribe to develop economic opportunities on the reservations.

The Southern Paiutes, now numbering roughly eleven thousand people, engage in cattle ranching, usually with tribal-owned herds, farming, and some tourism. They derive additional income by subletting tourist-oriented businesses on their reservations. There has also been a revival of Paiute crafts, particularly basketmaking, but many Paiutes still depend upon jobs off the reservations.

SOUTHERN UTE ENCAMPMENT, ALONG THE PINE RIVER NEAR IGNACIO, COLORADO, CIRCA 1900

COURTESY: ANIMAS MUSEUM, DURANGO, COLORADO   HISTORICAL PHOTOGRAPH: FRANK GONNER

The Utes

The Ute people once wandered an enormous and varied domain, encompassing mountains, plains, and desert, as they lived the seasonal round. Like all hunter-gatherers, they needed a huge area of land to support their way of life.

The Utes have long lived upon the Colorado Plateau and neighboring regions, like the Paiutes, to whom they are closely related, speaking a Shoshonean dialect of the Uto-Aztecan language and prior to the arrival of the Spaniards, living a fairly pure form of the seasonal round.

They believed in a supreme being, Manitou, the "Great Spirit," whose powers were associated with the sun. A bisexual male-female deity, Manitou created all life and all things and was, interestingly enough, also worshipped by the indigenous people of the Great Lakes region of the north-central United States. The Utes also believed in lesser gods, whose powers were subordinate to Manitou, and in life after death, when their spirits would travel to live with the sun in a place where there was no sickness, pain, or suffering—only happiness. The animals too, the Utes believed, went to the same paradise.

Every morning, when the Utes arose to begin the day, they faced the rising sun, took its warmth into their hands and "poured" the warmth over their bodies in ritual greeting. Religion for the Utes was an extremely personal experience involving oneness with the natural world and requiring no religious hierarchy to achieve that communion.

Perhaps the descendents of the early Fremont people or of a people who split off from the main body of the early Basketmaker Anasazi, the Utes may have been part of the long-ago Desert Archaic culture and may have lived in the Colorado Plateau region for ten thousand years or more. Or, they may be descendents of a nomadic people who filtered into the Southwest from the north while the Anasazi lived in the Four Corners area.

The Utes eventually occupied virtually all mountains of Colorado and are the longest con-

PREVIOUS PAGE: SANGRE DE CRISTO MOUNTAINS, GREAT SAND DUNES NATIONAL MONUMENT, COLORADO

79

tinuous residents of the state. They also inhabited most of Utah, which is named after them, and a small area of extreme southern Wyoming and part of extreme northern New Mexico.

In times past, as spring came, the Utes split into small family groups and followed deer and elk as the animals began to move into the high mountains for the summer. There the Utes remained, living off hunting and fishing, until wild plants began to reach maturity.

As the first touches of gold and orange tinged the aspens, the Utes moved back into the sheltered foothills or to the edge of the desert, often stopping along the way to harvest crops they had planted in the spring.

There in the low country, the individual families that had earlier dispersed came together to spend the winter with other families of their band, seven of which, at least in historical times, formed the Ute tribe. Each loosely structured band concentrated its movements within specific locales.

The Ute bands, together perhaps totaling upwards of ten thousand people, consisted of the Mouache band, living in southern Colorado and northern New Mexico along the Sangre de Cristo Mountains; the Capote band, living in the San Luis Valley in Colorado and along the Chama and Rio Grande rivers of extreme northern New Mexico, and the Weminuche, living in and near the San Juan Mountains of southwest Colorado and northwest New Mexico. There was also the Tabeguache or Uncompahgre, living in or near the northern San Juans; the Parianuc or Grand River Utes, living along the Colorado River in western Colorado and eastern Utah; the Yampa band, along the Yampa River in northwest Colorado; and the Uintah band, in the Uintah Basin in east-central Utah and the Wasatch and Uinta mountains of northeast Utah.

The Utes collectively called themselves, the Nuche, the "People," but the Shoshoni and Comanche people called them, Yuuttaa or Yutah, a term which has never been precisely translated. In the early seventeenth century, Spanish Governor Luis de Rosas of Santa Fe corrupted the Shoshoni and Comanche name and reported the capture of eighty "Uticahs," a term which eventually evolved to "Uintas," "Utahs," or "Utes."

When the members of the bands held their rendezvous in winter, it was a time of socializing after the isolation of the summer. Extended families reunited, friendships were renewed, goods were traded, social events were held.

During the summer, the Utes required little or no shelter, like other people of the Great Basin, using only wickiups, consisting of a frame of wooden poles covered with brush and reeds. In winter, they lived in tepees, an adaptation from the Plains Indians.

In spring, the Bear Dance, the most ancient Ute dance, was held when bears emerge from their dens after the winter hibernation. Depicted in ancient petroglyphs found in the Uinta Mountains of Utah and even in Fremont rock art, the Bear Dance was a social occasion of tremendous importance.

For three days and three nights, the dancers danced, face-to-face, men in a line to the north, women in a line to the south, within the boundary of a large circle. Finally, at noon on the third day, the women "pushed" the men from the circle to the north by dancing toward them. The dance then ended with a feast. It was also during the Bear Dance, immediately prior to the band again dispersing into the high country, that most marriages occurred.

Horses and Freedom

But a radical change came to this age-old way of life when the Utes acquired horses.

They had previously transported their possessions on travois, pulled by women or dogs to the next place of encampment. Such moves were a slow, arduous process.

Horses brought the Utes new mobility.

For the first time, they found it realistic to journey significant distances from the mountains to hunt the much-valued buffalo of the Great Plains. It was also possible to leave women and children in more distant and protected locales when engaging enemies in battle. But most important, it was no longer necessary for the Utes to scatter to hunt and to gather.

Because the people could remain together and develop greater cohesion and social structure, their leaders had more influence.

Like other Indians of the region, the Utes became raiders in earnest, attacking other tribes, especially Plains Indians and Navajos, as well as isolated ranches and small settlements in the Colorado and Utah mountains. From these, they took horses to ride, herd animals to eat, and cap-

ABOVE: CHIEF OURAY
COURTESY: COLORADO HISTORICAL SOCIETY

tives to sell as slaves.

The Ute culture, previously influenced mostly by the Desert culture, began to be much more profoundly influenced by the Plains culture, and to a lesser degree, by the cultures of the Pueblo and Navajo people.

But then came the 1850s and the beginning of the end of the Ute way of life.

Time of Sorrows

Gold was discovered at Cripple Creek, Colorado, near present-day Colorado Springs in the 1850s, sparking the Pike's Peak gold rush. Compounded by the extreme dislocations caused by the Civil War, hordes of miners and settlers swarmed into the Colorado Territory, then demanded the removal of Colorado Plains Indians and of the Utes.

At the beginning of the influx, the Ute chief Ouray—pronounced "YOU-ray" and meaning "Arrow"—predicted, "We shall fall as the leaves from the trees when winter comes, and the lands we have roamed for countless generations will be given to the miner and the plowshare...and we shall be buried out of sight."

Somehow Ouray, of the Uncompahgre band, was able to see the futility of the Ute's situation in the mid-nineteenth century and the implications of the sheer numbers of people about to descend upon his land.

The series of treaties made with the Utes and broken in rapid succession was perhaps one of the most profound examples of the lack of good faith extended by the United States toward the Indians.

As the Colorado Territory was settled, pressure grew for the removal of the Utes from twenty million acres of Colorado. Colorado Governor Frederick Pitkin said, "My idea is that unless removed by the government, they must be exterminated...." Simultaneously, covert warfare was waged upon the Indians, as hunters slaughtered the buffalo in the hopes that the animals' extinction would also mean the end of the Indians who depended upon them.

Many Plains Indians either lived or hunted at the time in eastern Colorado: Cheyenne, Arapahoe, Kiowas, Kiowa Apaches—an Apache group who had long ago settled with Kiowas living in the Black Hills of South Dakota—Shoshones, Pawnees, and Sioux.

Some attacked pioneer settlements in an attempt to drive out the strangers who were inundating their lands. Nonetheless, the Utes remained mostly at peace, in no small part due to the vision and determination of their half-Jicarilla Apache, half-Ute chief, Ouray. United States President Rutherford Hayes once said of him, "Ouray is the most intellectual man I have ever conversed with."

Meanwhile, under the Treaty of 1868, the Utes were forced to move well back from the population centers that had sprung up along Colorado's Front Range. This cost them the valuable parkland regions of central and northern Colorado, as well as the San Luis Valley in south-central Colorado. However, the remaining western portion of the state, approximately sixteen million acres, was to be theirs, according to the treaty, "for as long as the rivers run and the grasses grow," primarily because settlers considered those lands to be worthless.

However, only months later, gold was discovered in the San Juan Mountains, and the government, helpless to halt the influx of gold-obsessed prospectors, insisted that the Utes sign a new treaty ceding the San Juans. The Utes were probably lied to when they signed the agreement —the Brunot Treaty of 1873—likely believing that they were signing away only those lands with mines actually upon them.

In the late 1870s, public opinion was turned

EARLY UTE DOMAIN
BLACK CANYON OF THE GUNNISON NATIONAL MONUMENT, COLORADO

EARLY UTE DOMAIN, COLORADO NATIONAL MONUMENT, COLORADO

1864. Few of the Cheyenne or Arapaho survived, and in the belief that "nits make lice," even small children and infants were killed, their scalps taken to be hung on soldiers' belts as souvenirs.

When details of the attack finally emerged, there was a public outcry, particularly in the eastern United States, condemning the wholesale murder of the mostly unarmed people. However, the indignation resulted in few reforms of Indian policy, nor did it change attitudes which demanded removal of Indians from their native lands.

Meanwhile, on behalf of the Utes, Ouray tried to work constructively with authorities. He wanted his people to at least retain hunting rights to large areas of Utah and Colorado, even if they were denied access to more settled locales. With the Meeker incident, he correctly realized that his people would be forced onto reservations and denied even their old hunting grounds—and their freedom and self-sufficiency.

The Reservations

Finally in the 1880s, with many Coloradans galled that the Utes still occupied so much valuable land, yet another treaty was negotiated. It further reduced the Ute domain, relegating Colorado and northern New Mexico Utes to a 15 mile-wide, 140 mile-long parcel south of the San Juan Mountains, the so-called Ute Strip, running parallel to the Colorado-New Mexico border and in one area reaching slightly into northern New Mexico.

Meanwhile, most Utah Utes were forced onto the Uintah reservation east of Salt Lake City in the

even further against the Utes, when Indian agent Nathan Meeker and eight other men were killed in a Ute uprising at Meeker, Colorado.

Young Utes were angered that promised government supplies had not been delivered. Meeker inflamed the situation when he ordered a track for Ute horse racing plowed under. As the Utes became increasingly angry, he overreacted and sent for troops, escalating tensions until the Utes attacked, killing the men and taking three women and two children hostage for twenty-three days. Meanwhile, the troops summoned by Meeker were attacked and thirteen soldiers killed.

The Meeker uprising increased the outcry for the Utes' removal from Colorado—fear and hatred fanned in no small part by "yellow" journalism. Newspapers found that they could profit from sensationalizing and even blatantly distorting events. In print, Indians were invariably portrayed as villains, whites as virtuous heroes or put-upon victims.

The Meeker Massacre has lived in strange infamy in Colorado compared with the so-called Sand Creek "incident."

Although camped south of Pueblo, Colorado, in a full state of surrender, four hundred to five hundred mostly unarmed Cheyenne and Arapaho people were attacked by the volunteer army of the Colorado Territory, during the early morning hours of November 29,

EARLY UTE DOMAIN, DINOSAUR NATIONAL MONUMENT, COLORADO

early 1860s. Following the Meeker Massacre, the Yampa, Uncompahgre, and Grand River bands were removed to the Uintah reservation. However, because of overcrowding and resulting friction between the Utes, a separate section of the Uintah reservation, the Ouray extension, east of the Green River in the area of Desolation Canyon, was created for Colorado's Northern Utes, bringing the northern Utah reservation to a total of 1.3 million acres.

Life on the Utah reservation, a wind-blown, semi-desert region, represented a difficult transition for the Northern Utes, particularly the Uncompahgre band, who were used to the lush, green mountains and foothills of western Colorado.

From an enormous area spanning much of two states, the Utes were relegated to two comparatively small reservations. The old way was dead. There were no more valleys in which to hunt, no more fertile mountainsides upon which to harvest plants in the ways of old. Once one of the most self-sufficient people in the world, the Utes were relegated to handouts from the government.

But there was more infamy to come. In 1885 the Hunter Act passed Congress. It awarded private land ownership to individuals within the tribe for purposes of farming, usually 160 acres per family, lesser plots for individuals.

Then, to appease those who wanted even the reservations abolished, remaining lands were considered surplus and were opened to homesteading. Soon, even the Ute reservations were broken up and checkerboarded with the 160-acre plots of homesteaders.

Chief Ignacio of southwest Colorado's Weminuche band feared that such a policy would result in the destruction of the Weminuches'

Mexico, were protected for the Weminuche with a ban on homesteading.

Therefore, the Ute Strip was divided into two separate reservations, the Southern Ute reservation, headquartered out of Ignacio, Colorado, and consisting mostly of the Moache and Capote bands; and the western reservation, the Ute Mountain reservation with headquarters at Towoac, Colorado, and consisting mostly of the Weminuche band. Tragically, of the 810,000 acres the Southern Ute reservation originally encompassed, only 307,000 acres were left after homesteading.

Meanwhile, a small additional allotment of trust land and fee-patent land, eventually totaling close to six thousand acres, was created at White Mesa, south of Blanding, Utah, for a group of Weminuche Utes, who were determined to remain close to their native Blue Mountains. These lands, with about three hundred Utes on them, are administered as part of the Ute Mountain reservation.

The Present

UTE POTTERY FACTORY, UTE MOUNTAIN RESERVATION, TOWAOC, COLORADO

In 1950, under the Indian Claims Act of 1946, the Utes won court judgements totaling $43 million from the United States government for lands taken from them in the 1800s, money which was invested and now represent a significant source of tribal revenue. Other tribal income—some have even argued, wealth—is derived from energy leases on tribal property, as well as tourism and revenue from tribal-owned casinos

While the tribe is reluctant to release specifics, it has been reported that each Southern Ute tribal member over sixty, for example, receives a

TAOS PUEBLO, NEW MEXICO

Dawn of the New Millennium

Their cultures have survived here, sometimes for thousands of years, enduring despite the adversity of nature and, in recent centuries, the arrival of literally millions of newcomers to the Americas.

But what of the future of the Indians of the Colorado Plateau, a region experiencing rapid population growth, the spread of urbanization, and increasing competition for limited resources, especially water and land.

Despite the Colorado Plateau's appearance as a vast, under-populated place, it is in fact extremely crowded, with virtually every acre within its expanses spoken for—for grazing, energy development, recreation, housing development, as reservation, national parks, military bases, designated wilderness. The list goes on.

The area is particularly crowded in light of this region's aridity. Many of its aquifers are being mined, the water used faster than an aquifer can replenish itself. Many people believe the rivers are allocated far beyond what they will be able to deliver if a prolonged drought should return to the Southwest, as it inevitably will. In fact, the last twenty years are the dampest in the Southwest in the last two thousand, a trend unlikely to continue.

This is a frail land, prone to erosion, a land slow to heal the insults delivered to it, where the wagon tracks left by early settlers and the footpaths worn by the long-ago Anasazi, can still be seen.

In this rapidly growing and increasingly crowded land, cultures sometimes clash and people sometimes work at cross purposes.

Just north of Santa Fe, New Mexico, at the edge of the tiny village of Cuyamungue and just

*PREVIOUS PAGE: CANYONLANDS
NATIONAL PARK, UTAH
INSET: YOUNG GIRLS, SAN JUAN PUEBLO,
NEW MEXICO*

a mile or so beyond the eastern boundary of the Colorado Plateau, a 250-foot cellular communications tower looms above the piñon- and juniper-carpeted foothills of the Sangre de Cristo Mountains. That recently erected tower—called a blight on the New Mexico landscape by Santa Fe county officials and some area residents—is perhaps a symbol of the conflicts and quandaries facing the region.

County officials charged that the communications company owning the tower deliberately leased land from Nambé Pueblo—Indian reservation exempt from state and county laws—to circumvent zoning regulations which would have prohibited the tower's installation. The county officials called the company and Nambé insensitive to Santa Fe County's efforts to prevent urban blight along the scenic corridor between Santa Fe and Pojoaque.

HOGAN, MONUMENT VALLEY NAVAJO TRIBAL PARK, ARIZONA

The officials warned that if other pueblos followed suit, it would impede attempts to direct growth in an area which, if current projections hold, will experience a population doubling by 2020 and a four-fold increase by 2050, a population of more than half-a-million in an area that as recently as 1970 had only about fifty thousand people.

But Nambé officials, while reluctant to engage in a debate, said the goal was not to create an eyesore, but to seek economic self-sufficiency for the pueblo—a daunting task in the face of funding cuts to Indian tribes by the federal government and at a time when Nambé, unlike many neighboring pueblos, has turned its back on Indian gaming, a new and controversial dimension to life on Indian reservations.

Indian-owned casinos have brought prosperity to many pueblos and tribes, although critics charge it has also brought crime, hurt nearby businesses, deprived state and local governments of income by diverting money away from purchases that would generate sales tax revenue, and encouraged those who are already poor to gamble—sometimes using their welfare checks.

But the tribes argue that the casinos give them financial security and opportunities. The tribal-owned gaming houses, they argue, provide money for college educations for the tribes' children, pay for needed services and police protection, provide well-paying jobs to tribal members and others, and generate employment opportunities and revenue for tribal investments.

State governments, they add, under gaming compacts, usually receive some revenue from the casinos.

And there are the Indians' concerns about what others are doing to them and their traditional lands.

Also north of Santa Fe, near the tiny Hispanic farming community of Lyden and the Indian pueblo of San Juan, stands Black Mesa, a huge basalt-lined promontory along the west side of the Rio Grande north of Española. The basalt boulders on this twelve mile-long, four mile-wide mesa are strewn with literally thousands of petroglyphs, carved over the last five thousand years into the black patina oxidized onto the basalt's surface.

Some archeologists say the Black Mesa petroglyphs—perhaps up to twenty thousand—represent one of the most spectacular collections in the Southwest.

The petroglyphs seem to be everywhere, petroglyphs of animals, serpents, suns, stars, what may be dragonflies or butterflies, symbols perhaps signifying water, and dozens of others upon which one can only gaze and wonder—especially since some experts believe the meaning of petroglyphs evolves and changes over time, as does language.

The more elaborate petroglyphs were probably carved by the Basketmaker Anasazi roughly two thousand years ago, or more recently, by the Renaissance, or Pueblo IV, Anasazi, which would have included the nearby residents of the huge Poshuouinge and other pueblos between 1300 and 1600 A.D. Other petroglyphs at the site, ancient and now barely discernable, were carved by some long-ago hunter-gathers, who visited the mesa five thousand or more years ago.

The tenets of their faith keep the people of San Juan Pueblo from elaborating on the significance of the petroglyphs, but they say the rock art is sacred to them and vital to their religion.

San Juan residents have watched aghast in recent years as part of Black Mesa, including one section where it is believed a twelve-foot-long serpent petroglyph rested, was strip mined by a local gravel pit operator for boulders used to stabilize the banks of a nearby U.S. Bureau of Reclamation reservoir—mining probably done in violation of federal environmental and antiquities laws.

Petroglyph National Monument immediately west of Albuquerque, meanwhile, is threatened by a proposal to put a highway through part of the monument, despite the protests of environmentalists and Indian spiritual leaders.

The list of offenses seems endless.

Related mining operations near San Juan Pueblo caused further problems, as dozens of forty-ton, large-haul trucks—San Juan claimed traveling at excessive speeds—almost daily cut through the community as they rushed from mine to mill.

Finally, tribal officials imposed a mandatory fourteen-ton weight limit on its portion of New Mexico 582—a road in many places little more than ten-feet wide—and sent tribal police to enforce a crackdown, effectively closing the road and the mine it served, but not without hard feelings on the part of the mostly Hispanic truckers.

The Hopi, meanwhile, believe that water pumped from their sacred Black Mesa in northern Arizona to slurry coal—strip mined over the protests of tribal traditionalists—through a pipe to a distant power plant in Nevada is causing declining water levels in springs that have for centuries provided reliable water for the villagers and their crops.

Other Indians have been left with a legacy of radiation and nuclear wastes from Cold War-era uranium mining and refining on the Colorado Plateau.

Laguna Pueblo reached a settlement with Anaconda Minerals in which the company, at a cost of $45 million, filled three enormous pits—hiring a Laguna Pueblo-owned construction company to do the work—where uranium was mined until 1982.

Prior to the cleanup, however, radioactive dust from the mines often blew over the pueblo.

The reclaimed area will be monitored, but the use of at least three thousand acres—for grazing, housing, or farming—will likely be restricted indefinitely, Laguna officials say. Another nearby open-pit uranium mine—in the same formation, but on Spanish grant land—remains unreclaimed and, officials fear, may be polluting nearby precious water supplies.

Some Navajos, meanwhile, have raised concerns that tribal timber operations in the Chuska Mountains are removing timber at above sustainable levels and that, despite attempts at reclamation, extensive strip mining by off-reservation interests is leaving permanent environmental damage on huge tracts of the reservation.

But perhaps a greater threat to the native cultures is simply time and the constant pressure of a surrounding, predominant industrial society, which with its mass media, pop culture, and overpowering pervasiveness has reached even into isolated regions, such as Supai village—reached only by helicopter or horseback—at the bottom of the Grand Canyon.

Children of the Hopi, Navajo, Ute, and other tribes, like children everywhere, are often more interested in the latest computer game or fashion trend than they are in learning ancient and, to them, sometimes irrelevant traditions. And, as almost everywhere in the United States today, juvenile crime, drugs, and teen pregnancy are a problem on the reservations.

American Indians are more than twice as likely to fall victim to violent crime, the United States Justice Department reported in 1999, while a 1997 study by federal law-enforcement officials and tribal leaders declared a public safety crisis on the reservations and proposed doubling the size of reservation police forces.

ZUNI PUEBLO DANCERS

Indians in the 1990s suffered violent crimes—murders, rapes, assaults, robberies—at 124 per every 100,000 people, more than twice as often as the national average, while child abuse—or at least the reporting of child abuse—soared. Meanwhile, roughly four percent of the Indian population, versus two percent of Anglos, are somehow under the jurisdiction of the criminal justice system.

Authorities are at a loss to explain why, but the increase may be driven in part by a proliferation of gangs and a lack of law enforcement, especially on often-sprawling and isolated reservations. The 1997 study, for example, found only 1,600 tribal and Bureau of Indian Affairs officers patrolling over 56 million acres, while on the enormous Navajo reservation, there is often only one officer—who must patrol, on average, ten thousand square miles alone—for every one thousand residents.

Many tribes, meanwhile, are struggling just to keep their language alive, asking tribal elders to record their languages and create dictionaries for fear the languages will otherwise someday be completely forgotten.

While there are increasing economic opportunities on the reservations—at the casinos, in tribal-run industries or businesses, in tribal government or construction—these often do not keep pace with a population growth rate hovering near three children per woman, a rate that will double the size of many tribes within a generation.

Some Indians still must work off the reservations, or chose to do so, in Albuquerque, Santa Fe, Phoenix, Salt Lake, Denver.

A major employer for many of the Pueblos of the Rio Grande Valley is Los Alamos National Laboratory, where the first atomic bombs were developed during World War II. Along with its subcontractors, the laboratory employs an estimated nine thousand people in nuclear weapons and related work.

But, there is still a resiliency to the Indian cultures, reflected in the abundance of color.

That color is visible in the clothing and creations of Indians gathered on the Plaza in Santa Fe, the turquoise and silver jewelry they sell spread out under the *portal* of the Palace of the Governors, an adobe structure dating from the Spanish occupation.

Color is almost palpable on the feast days, when every able-bodied person in a pueblo—from tots barely old enough to walk, to elders with stooped shoulders—don traditional attire and dance for hours to the ancient one-two beat of a deep, resonating drum.

The women are particularly beautiful, clad in traditional costumes of knee-high moccasins, calf-length dresses, with brightly colored scarves draped around their shoulders and, sometimes, traditional pots or square-shaped head dresses perched on their jet-black hair.

The people move with profound dignity, sometimes with boughs of evergreen held reverently in front of them, hundreds of human beings moving in columns in timed unison, one huge group in one part of the pueblo, followed by another in another part—an enormous community of sound, color, movement, like one great, structured flock of birds moving in dignified concert.

In Monument Valley, color is expressed by a Navajo woman—clad in a turquoise-colored velvet skirt and maroon blouse embellished with turquoise jewelry—moving a small herd of churro sheep across a sand dune to the safety of a corral for the night; or a Navajo girl, her blue velvet skirt fanned out around her, sitting on the sand as a tourist takes her picture; or a Navajo man riding his horse at a dead run across the desert near the ruins of Chaco Canyon; or a traditional Navajo weaver patiently working yarn at a loom at Two Gray Hills in the foothills of the Chuska Mountains.

And there is an old Hopi man—his face a road map of wrinkles and a bright blue headband confining his salt-and-pepper gray hair—as he pauses in the coolness of the dawn to look toward the San Francisco Peaks in the distance, before making his way through the winding streets of Oraibi on his way to the kiva to pray.

Yes, the Colorado Plateau and its people are truly far more beautiful and colorful than fiction could ever be.

LEFT MITTEN, RIGHT MITTEN, MERRICK BUTTE
MONUMENT VALLEY NAVAJO TRIBAL PARK